Teach Yourself VISUALLY™

Piano

Hear Audio Tracks from This Book at wiley.com!

In case you need a little help in understanding how a particular piece is supposed to sound, we've included audio tracks from this book on our Web site. You can access those files via this link: www.wiley.com/go/tyvpiano. Here's a list of the tracks that you'll find there:

Teach Yourself VISUALLY™

Piano

Visual®

by Mary Sue Taylor and Tere Stouffer

WILEY

Wiley Publishing, Inc.

Library of Congress Control Number: 2005939198

ISBN-13: 978-0-471-74990-5
ISBN-10: 0-471-74990-7

Printed in the United States of America

10 9 8 7 6 5 4 3 2 1

Book production by Wiley Publishing, Inc. Composition Services

Praise for the Teach Yourself VISUALLY Series

I just had to let you and your company know how great I think your books are. I just purchased my third Visual book (my first two are dog-eared now!) and, once again, your product has surpassed my expectations. The expertise, thought, and effort that go into each book are obvious, and I sincerely appreciate your efforts. Keep up the wonderful work!

—Tracey Moore (Memphis, TN)

I have several books from the Visual series and have always found them to be valuable resources.

—Stephen P. Miller (Ballston Spa, NY)

Thank you for the wonderful books you produce. It wasn't until I was an adult that I discovered how I learn—visually. Although a few publishers out there claim to present the material visually, nothing compares to Visual books. I love the simple layout. Everything is easy to follow. And I understand the material! You really know the way I think and learn. Thanks so much!

—Stacey Han (Avondale, AZ)

Like a lot of other people, I understand things best when I see them visually. Your books really make learning easy and life more fun.

—John T. Frey (Cadillac, MI)

I am an avid fan of your Visual books. If I need to learn anything, I just buy one of your books and learn the topic in no time. Wonders! I have even trained my friends to give me Visual books as gifts.

—Illona Bergstrom (Aventura, FL)

I write to extend my thanks and appreciation for your books. They are clear, easy to follow, and straight to the point. Keep up the good work! I bought several of your books and they are just right! No regrets! I will always buy your books because they are the best.

—Seward Kollie (Dakar, Senegal)

Credits

Acquisitions Editor
Pam Mourouzis

Project Editor
Suzanne Snyder

Technical Editor
Martha Thieme

Editorial Manager
Christina Stambaugh

Publisher
Cindy Kitchel

Vice President and Executive Publisher
Kathy Nebenhaus

Interior Design
Kathie Rickard
Elizabeth Brooks

Cover Design
José Almaguer

Interior Photography
Matt Bowen

Dedication

To my daughter, Valerie Rehm. She is a photographer in Seattle. She has a passion for nature and travels to many beautiful locations capturing the beauty of the earth. She has been a great encouragement to me in my writing of this book.

—Mary Sue Taylor

Special Thanks...

Thanks to Meridian Music in Carmel, Indiana, especially President Craig Gigax, for providing the location for many of the photos in this book.

About the Authors

Mary Sue Taylor has taught beginning piano, jazz, improvisation, chord study, and other related topics a diverse array of students since 1956. She has also filled her share of musical requests, having played piano in the Atlanta area since 1954. Over the years, she has dusted the keys of nearly every piano in the Atlanta area, from formal society clubs to dim, smoke-filled jazz bars to the hottest house parties. She lives in Roswell, Georgia, with her husband, Jimmy.

Tere Stouffer is a freelance author and editor who has now broken into the double digits—this is her tenth book. She lives in Knoxville, Tennessee, with her chocolate Lab, Maxine, who kept her feet warm on many a late winter night spent working on this manuscript.

Acknowledgments

Writing any book takes an amazing team of people, and this book was no different. We give a heart-felt thanks for acquisitions editor Pam Mourouzis, who championed this book and got us started. Project editor Suzanne Snyder then took over the project and couldn't have been a better fit for us: With a musicology degree, she was a tremendous help when we struggled to explain challenging topics. She and editorial manager Christina Stambaugh patiently organized and edited not only the text but also hundreds of photos and pieces of music. Our photographer, Matt Bowen, was responsible for the beautiful photos throughout the book.

Table of Contents

chapter 3 Steps and Intervals

chapter 4 Dynamics and Tempo

chapter 5 — **Warming Up**

chapter 6 — Chords

 **Meter, Harmony, and Movement**

chapter **8** **Advanced Musical Terms**

chapter 9 Advanced Chords

chapter 10 Musical Styles

The Piano

To activate sound on a piano, you press a key, which releases a small hammer that strikes a string. The string then vibrates with sound, which is called a *note.* To reduce this vibration and soften the sound, you press on a pedal.

The History of the Piano

The piano was invented in the early eighteenth century by Bartolomeo Cristofori of Florence, Italy. Cristofori's job was to design and maintain the keyboard instruments used in the court of Prince Ferdinand de' Medici. John Brent of Philadelphia built the first piano in the United States in 1774.

Cristofori was a maker of harpsichords and clavichords (the two predecessors of the piano), so it is reasonable that his instrument would be similar to these instruments, but—instead—capable of softness and loudness. Harpsichords are neither soft nor loud; nor can they produce much of a sustained tone. This is because the strings of the harpsichord are plucked with quills or plectra. Clavichords are more like pianos, in that the strings are struck with metal tangents. The tone produced by a clavichord, however, is soft. Cristofori's invention used hammers to hit the strings. Depending on the pianist's touch at the keyboard, a key could be pressed lightly (producing a soft tone), or struck with enough force that it produced a loud tone. And, unlike both the harpsichord and the clavichord, a tone could be sustained on the piano, depending on the pianist's desire. Cristofori's original name for the piano was *gravicembalo col piano e forte*, which means "harpsichord with soft and loud."

Cristofori's invention soon became known as the *fortepiano*, which distinguished the eighteenth-century instrument from its predecessors and today's piano, the full name of which is the *pianoforte*. Cristofori's early fortepiano had one relatively thin string per note and was much softer than today's pianos. By Mozart's time, it had two strings per note and the hammers were covered in leather. A German organ builder named Gottfried Silbermann began making fortepianos in the 1730s. He is responsible for adding a forerunner of today's damper pedal, which you will be learning about later in this chapter.

The eighteenth-century fortepiano keyboard often didn't look the way the piano's keyboard looks today. Many fortepianos had keyboards that resembled the keyboard of the harpsichord of the time, in which the white keys were black and the black keys were white.

In the nineteenth century, the piano underwent many changes. The frame changed from wood to iron, enabling strings to become thicker and strung with more tension without breaking. (String breakage had been a problem: Beethoven was constantly hitting keys with such force that strings broke.) More strings were added and more octaves. You'll learn about octaves later in this book. The hammers were covered with felt to achieve better tone quality from the new steel strings. At this point, let's leave the subject of the history of the piano and look at how today's piano is constructed.

The Sounding Board

The piano's sounding board, an internal part of the piano that you normally can't see unless you have a baby grand or grand piano with the lid up, has four parts: strings of different sizes, pins, hammers, and dampers.

What's Inside

The hammers strike the strings, and the vibration of the strings may be dampened (that is, reduced) by the dampers. The pedals, discussed in the following section, allow the player to alter the string vibration.

The thickest, longest strings produce the deepest and most resonant sounds, while thinner, shorter strings produce higher, less resonant sounds. The lowest range of the piano uses one string per tone; the middle range uses two strings for more resonance; and the highest range uses three strings for even more resonance. The very highest range needs all the help it can get to resonate, so there are no dampers there. The pins are the little metal objects that are used to tune the strings.

Pedals

There are three pedals on the piano: the damper pedal, the soft pedal, and the sostenuto pedal. The pedals are found at the bottom of the piano, below the keyboard, and you push them with your feet.

Types of Pedals

DAMPER PEDAL

The right-most pedal is called the *damper pedal* or *loud pedal* and is used more than the other two pedals. It's called a *damper*, because it holds the dampers up, preventing them from dampening the strings, thus letting the strings ring until you release (lift your foot off) the pedal. In this way, the damper pedal enables you to sustain notes as you play.

SOFT PEDAL

The left-most pedal is the *soft pedal,* and on the grand piano it softens the sound of notes by shifting the keyboard slightly to the right so that the hammers hit one less string in the middle and high ranges (see the "What's Inside" section, earlier). For this reason, the soft pedal is sometimes also called the *una corda,* which is Italian for "one string." On upright pianos, the soft pedal works differently, but it still softens the sound of the notes.

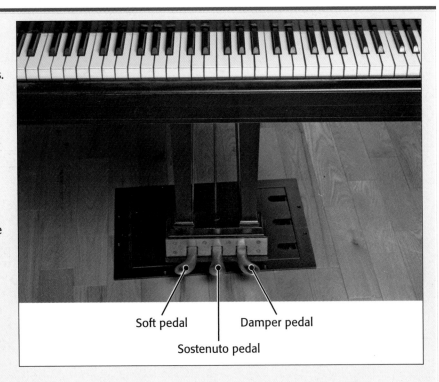

Soft pedal   Damper pedal

Sostenuto pedal

SOSTENUTO PEDAL

The middle pedal is the *sostenuto* (sus-tah-*new*-toe) *pedal* and is not used as much as the other two. Sostenuto is Italian for "sustained," which makes sense because—like the damper pedal—this pedal holds the dampers above a specific note or notes you want to sustain. You can, meanwhile, use the other pedals at the same time and it won't affect the notes being sustained by the sostenuto pedal.

Note that many less expensive upright pianos do not have a sostenuto pedal, but instead have a *practice pedal* that muffles the sound so that you can play without disturbing your neighbors if you live in an apartment or if it is late at night. Virtually all grand pianos have a sostenuto pedal, as do some of the more expensive uprights.

How and When to Use the Pedals

Push a pedal *after* you've struck the keys (this produces a cleaner sound and is called *syncopated pedaling*). Overpedaling results in notes that sound muddled.

The music shown here gives you pedaling instructions: You'll use the damper pedal, since it is the pedal most commonly used by beginning piano players. Hold the damper pedal down when the line is continued, and release the damper pedal when the line stops at a small notch. Hold the damper pedal again when the line begins again.

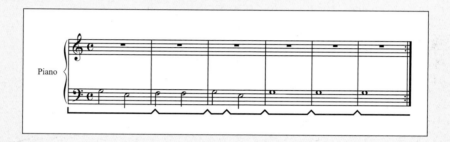

The piano has 88 keys: 52 white keys and 36 black keys.

GROUPS OF TWO BLACK KEYS

Notice the groups of two black keys. Starting at the far left side of the keyboard (the *bottom*), press both black keys at the same time. Do the same *up* the keyboard (toward the right).

There are three white keys—C, D, and E—by the two black keys. Starting at the bottom of the keyboard, press all the Cs. The Cs are left of the first black key in each two-black-key grouping.

Now press all the Ds—the key between the two black keys in each group. Then press all the Es, the key to the right of the second black key in each two-black-key group.

GROUPS OF THREE BLACK KEYS

The rest of the black keys are in groups of three. Find the first group of three black keys at the bottom of the keyboard, and play them all the way up.

There are four white keys by the three black keys, and these are the notes F, G, A, and B. Again, playing only white keys, press all the F keys (to the left of the first black key of the three-black-key groups). The Gs are the next white key to the right of all the Fs. The As are the next white key to the right of all the Gs. And the Bs are the next white key to the right of all the As.

THE KEYS IN AN OCTAVE

You have now played and learned the eight notes that comprise the piano octave: C, D, E, F, G, A, B, and C again. (An *octave* is eight notes, so when you play one C key, and then play another C key up or down the keyboard, you play an octave higher or lower, respectively.)

The black keys have names, too—they're sharps and flats. See Chapter 2 for details.

Finding Middle C

Put your right thumb on the C key closest to the middle of the keyboard (called *middle C*). One octave down from middle C is known as *low C*, while one octave up from middle C is known as *high C*.

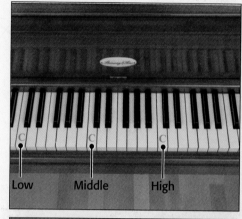

Play middle C four times with your thumb. Now move up and play G four times with your pinky. Again play four Cs, and then play four Gs. Repeat this several times, saying the names of the notes out loud, until it feels comfortable. Now mix the keys, playing C once, G once, C once, and so on. You can also move down an octave and play C and G again. Keep playing C and G all over the keyboard.

With your left hand, place your thumb on middle C. Play C four times. Reach your pinky down the keyboard to F and play it four times. Again, repeat many times, saying the names of the notes as you strike the keys. Alternate C and F over and over, and then play the C and F combination all over the keyboard.

As you become comfortable playing these key combinations, use the damper pedal, and then the soft pedal, to see what difference those two pedals make in how the notes sound.

CONTINUED ON NEXT PAGE

Positioning Your Fingers

With your right hand, position your fingers on the keyboard as shown:

- C: Thumb (called 1)
- D: First finger (called 2)
- E: Middle finger (called 3)
- F: Ring finger (called 4)
- G: Pinky (called 5)

With your left hand, position your fingers on the keyboard as shown:

- C: Thumb (called 1)
- B: First finger (called 2)
- A: Middle finger (called 3)
- G: Ring finger (called 4)
- F: Pinky (called 5)

Practice these finger positions, saying the numbers to yourself in the beginning, and then progressing to note names.

TIP

One important tip that we could mention in every chapter of this book is that you want to watch the *music* instead of your fingers as you play. After you position your fingers on the keys, play the notes one at a time without looking, and you'll develop a feel for your position. As you progress in your playing abilities, if you find that you can't stop watching your fingers as you play, ask someone to hold a piece of paper over your hands to block your view.

An Exercise: The Alphabet Song

You can now play a piece. Place your right thumb on middle C and follow the notation and fingering shown on each line of the chart below. HC stands for high C. Watch your fingering, especially where your thumb crosses under your third finger.

1	2	3	1	2	3	4	5
C	D	E	F	G	A	B	HC
1	3	2	4	3	5	4	2
C	E	D	F	E	G	F	D
5	4	2	3	1	4	3	2
G	F	D	E	C	F	E	D
1	2	3	1	2	3	4	5
C	D	E	F	G	A	B	HC

Now come down from high C to middle C, as shown on each line of the chart below, watching your fingering.

5	4	3	2	1	3	2	1
HC	B	A	G	F	E	D	C
5	3	4	2	3	1	2	
HC	A	B	G	A	F	G	
5	2	3	2	4	3	2	
HC	G	A	G	B	A	G	
5	4	3	2	1	3	2	1
HC	B	A	G	F	E	D	C

CONTINUED ON NEXT PAGE

Now start with middle C and stretch up to high C with your fifth finger, as shown on the chart below. Rotate back and forth to get the feel of this eight-key spread.

Note: *In the chart, HC stands for high C.*

1	5	1	5	1	5	1	5
C	HC	C	HC	C	HC	C	HC
1	5	1	5	1	5	5	1
C	HC	C	HC	C	HC	HC	C

With your left hand, place your thumb on middle C and follow the notation and fingering shown. Watch your fingering, especially where your thumb crosses under, and your third finger crosses over.

Note: *In the chart, LC stands for low C.*

1	2	3	1	2	3	4	5
C	B	A	G	F	E	D	LC
1	3	2	4	3	5	4	
C	A	B	G	A	F	G	
1	4	3	4	2	3	4	
C	G	A	G	B	A	G	
1	2	3	1	2	3	4	5
C	B	A	G	F	E	D	LC

Now place your thumb on middle C and your fifth finger on low C, as shown. Again, rotate back and forth to get the feel of this eight-key spread.

1	5	1	5	1	5	1	5
C	LC	C	LC	C	LC	C	LC
5	1	5	1	5	1	1	5
LC	C	LC	C	LC	C	C	LC
1	1	5	5	1	5	5	1
C	C	LC	LC	C	LC	LC	C

FAQ

Why do I have to do the "thumb under" and the "3rd finger over" exercises? That is hard to do. Why are all these fingerings important?

We have only five fingers on each hand. Think about the number of notes you need to play from the first note to the last note. Unless you can grow more fingers, you won't have enough fingers to cover all the notes you need to play. That is why you need to do the "thumb under" and "3rd finger over" techniques, which free up more fingers to use. If you don't use proper fingering from the start, you will never be able to play accurately with any speed. There aren't any shortcuts.

Playing Position, Posture, and Hand Position

Good playing position, posture, and hand position are necessary when playing the piano. They keep your muscles from getting tired and sore as you play.

Position Yourself to Play Comfortably

PLAYING POSITION

Playing position refers to how you situate yourself in front of your piano, before you begin playing. Just as you adjust your computer workstation before you begin typing, you'll want to adjust your body and piano stool to achieve the greatest comfort level possible.

Be sure you're sitting facing the middle of the keyboard, so that all the keys are within easy reach. Pull your stool in far enough so that your knees are under

the keyboard. Adjust your piano stool so that your forearms (the part of your arm that runs from your elbow to your hands) are parallel to the keyboard. Place your feet flat on the floor, but still within reach of the pedals. Photo a shows bad foot placement. Photo b is correct foot placement.

POSTURE

Using good posture when playing the piano means keeping your shoulders lowered and pulled back.

One common posture mistake is to raise your shoulders (usually because your piano stool is too low, making the keyboard too high). This creates tension in your neck that will likely lead to soreness and discomfort in your neck, arms, and back.

A second common problem is to round your back as you play (see photo a). This usually occurs because your piano stool is too far from the keyboard, forcing you to slump as you play. Photo b shows correct posture.

HAND POSITION

The correct way to hold your hands on the piano is as though you have a golf ball in your hand. Pretend you're holding the golf ball, with your fingers loosely formed around it. You then press keys with the pads of your fingers (see photo b). Do not flatten your fingers out (as in photo a), because this slows your execution of the notes.

Look at the illustration to see how your hand should curve over the notes.

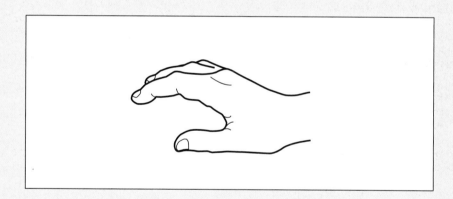

2

Reading Music and Playing Notes

Piano music is written on *manuscript paper* with two sets of lines and spaces. Each set is called a staff. Together, both sets are called the *grand* or *great staff.* The upper set is for the right hand, and the lower set is for the left hand.

Each staff contains five lines and four spaces. The lines and spaces represent notes on the piano. (Ignore, for now, the symbol that looks like a big C. You'll learn about it later in this chapter.)

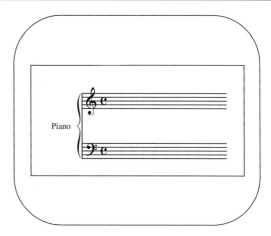

Components of the Staff

TREBLE CLEF

At the far left of the upper staff is a *treble clef sign.* The treble clef directs you to play the notes on this staff with your *right* hand only.

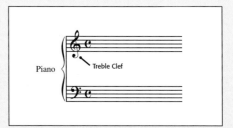

BASS CLEF

At the far left of the lower staff is a *bass clef sign.* The bass clef directs you to play the notes on this staff with the *left* hand only.

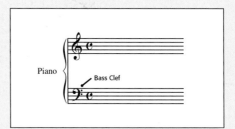

MEASURES AND BAR LINES

Measures are the areas between the *bar lines.* The bar lines separate one measure from another. You're allowed a certain number of beats within each measure.

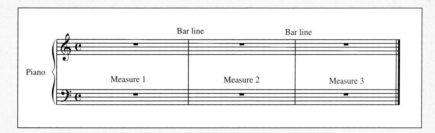

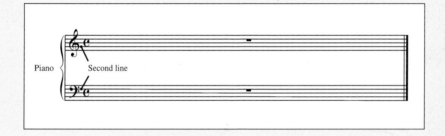

Notice that the middle section of the treble clef symbol curls around the second line (counting up) of the treble staff. The treble clef gets its alternate name from the name of this line.

Notice also that the two dots of the bass clef symbol straddle the second line (counting down) of the bass clef. The bass clef gets its alternate name from the name of this line.

On the following page, you'll learn the names of these two lines and, thus, the alternate names for the treble clef and the bass clef!

Notes on the Staff

On the staff are notes to tell you what to play. Each note gives you two pieces of information—which key to play and how long to hold each note before you play the next one.

Relating Notes to Piano Keys

RIGHT HAND

For the right hand (the treble clef), the slogan "Every Good Boy Does Fine" represents the notes on the five lines (E, G, B, D, F). Therefore, the treble clef's alternate name is the G clef. The word "FACE" represents the four spaces (F, A, C, E).

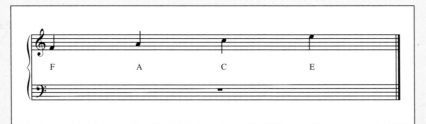

LEFT HAND

For the left hand (the bass clef), the slogan "Girls Bake Delicious Fudge Always" represents the notes on the five lines (G, B, D, F, A). The bass clef's alternate name is the F clef. The slogan "All Cars Eat Gas" represents the four spaces (A, C, E, G).

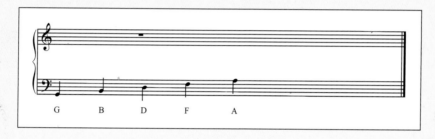

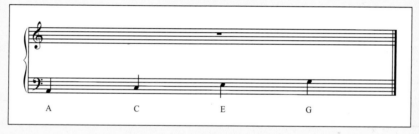

CONTINUED ON NEXT PAGE

Note Counts

WHOLE NOTES

A *whole note* is a white (unfilled) note head without a *stem* (a line extending from the note head). A whole note lasts four counts. In this example, the E key would be played for four counts, which means you strike the key once and hold it for a count of four.

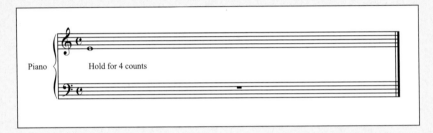

HALF NOTES

A *half note* is a white note head with a stem. A half note lasts two counts. Here, the G key is played twice for two counts each.

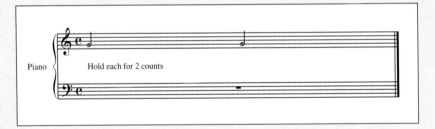

QUARTER NOTES

A *quarter note* is a black note head with a stem. A quarter note lasts one count. In the example shown, you play the F key four times for one count each.

EIGHTH NOTES

An eighth note is a black note with a *flag stem* (a stem with an extra squiggle on the side). It lasts one-half count. Here, you play E seven times for a total of three-and-a-half counts, and then an eighth rest for the last half count (see "Rests" later on this page).

When two or more eighth notes are next to each other, a bar is placed above them, as shown here.

DOTTED HALF NOTES

A half note with a dot after it is called a *dotted half note.* It lasts three counts. A dot after a note always gives the note an additional one-half of the value of the regular note. So, because a half note has two counts, the dot adds one more count (one half of two is one), for a total of three counts. The quarter rest adds one count.

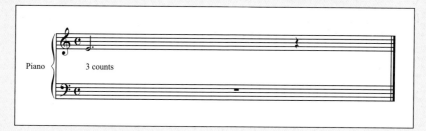

RESTS

Rests are markings that tell you to observe silence. They are measurements of time, just like notes. A whole rest tells you to rest for four counts (that is, be silent for four counts). A half rest requires two counts of silence, while a quarter rest requires one count of silence. An eighth rest, as you saw earlier, is a half count of silence.

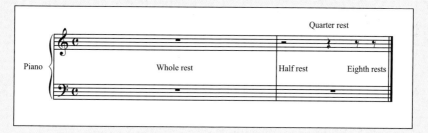

Sharps, Flats, and Naturals

The black keys take their names from the surrounding white keys, by adding "sharp" or "flat" to the white-key note names.

Sharps

Sharps are signs that appear right before the note you are playing that look like this: ♯.

A sharp tells you to play the black note just *up* from the white note with that name. So, a C♯ is the black note just up from C; that is, it's just between C and D.

Note that there is no B♯ black key, because there is no black key between B and C. Likewise, there is no E♯ black key, because there is no black key between E and F.

Whether on the treble clef (right-hand) or bass clef (left-hand) portion of the staff, a sharp sign before a note usually tells you to play the black key just to the right of the white key portrayed by the note.

Note the example, which shows C♯, D♯, F♯, and G♯.

Flats

Flats are little signs that look like this: ♭.

A flat note tells you to do just the opposite of the sharp: You move *down* the keyboard to the next black key.

Notice the example, which, in the first measure, asks you to place a whole E. In the second measure, it directs you to play a whole E♭.

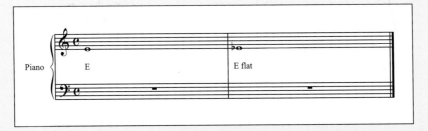

Natural Signs

A natural sign cancels out a sharp or flat, when necessary. This simply means to go back to the original white key and do not flat or sharp the note by playing the black key. The use of the natural sign will make more sense as you move along in your playing.

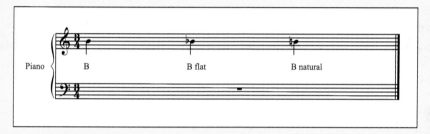

Notice the example, which shows a few measures of notes: G, F♯, F♮, E in the first measure; D, E♭, E♮, F in the second measure; F♯, F♮, F♯, F♮ in the third measure; and E♭, E♮ in the fourth measure.

TIP

An *accidental* is a sharp or flat note that's not part of the key signature. (You'll learn about key signatures in the next section.) The sharp or flat sign will appear in front of a particular note and sharps or flats that note for the entire measure (unless there is a natural that ends it). In the next measure the old key signature applies. You see some accidentals in your upcoming exercises.

Key Signature and Time Signature

In this section, you find out how to determine which "key" you're playing in (which is different from which key on the piano you're playing). When you look at a piece of music, at the very left of the first measure, you'll see two important signatures: the key signature and the time signature.

Key Signature

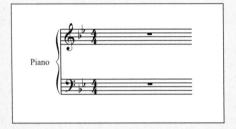

The *key signature* consists of sharps or flats on certain lines or spaces, located right at the beginning of the staff—after the treble or bass clef sign. The key signature tells you what key the piece is written in, a concept that's covered in Chapter 9. For now, just be aware that the key signature will appear in music, and it will tell you valuable information about the piece.

The key signature gives you the game rules for the entire piece (or at least until the key signature changes). If the key signature shows an F♯, all Fs will be sharped throughout the piece unless an F♮ in the form of an accidental overrides the F♯ for a measure (see **Tip** on the previous page). If B♭ and E♭ are shown, all Bs and Es are flatted—unless overridden by a B♮ or E♮ accidental for a measure.

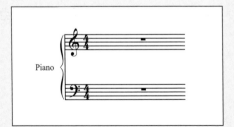

Note that, when you don't see any sharp or flat after the treble or bass clef signs, there is still a key signature. The absence of a sharp or flat is telling you to play in the key of C (meaning no sharps or flats).

Time Signature

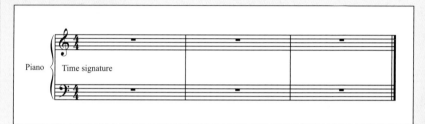

The *time signature* is always at the beginning of the staff just after the key signature. It's usually two numbers, one over the other.

The top number tells you how many counts (or beats) to a measure. 4/4 is the most common time signature, and it means that each measure will have four beats. This means that all the notes in the measure should add up to four beats (one whole note, two half notes, a half note and two quarter notes, four quarter notes, eight eighth notes, four eighth notes and a half note, and so on). When you see quarter notes in 4/4 time, count each as one beat. That's simple enough. But when you see half notes in 4/4 time, add an "and" between each beat to make sure you hold each note the right amount of time (1-and-2-and is the proper timing for a half note). Similarly, when you see a whole note in 4/4 time, hold it for four counts(1-and-2-and-3-and-4-and) before playing the next note.

Although 4/4 is the most common (for this reason, it is sometimes represented by a big C, standing for *common time*), many other time signatures are used. A waltz, for example, is always 3/4, which means there are three beats to each measure.

Remember, it's the top number that determines the number of beats to a measure. If it's 4/4 time, the combination of notes in the measure will add up to 4 beats. If it's 3/4 time, there are 3 beats to the measure.

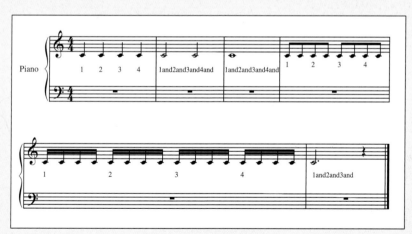

CONTINUED ON NEXT PAGE

The bottom number, the *value ratio,* tells you what kind of note gets one beat, or count.

The most common value ratio is 4, which means that a quarter note gets one beat. It follows, then, that a half note gets two beats, a dotted half note gets three beats, a whole note gets four beats, and an eighth note gets one-half beat.

If the value ratio is 8, an eighth note gets one beat. It then follows that a quarter note gets two beats, a half note gets four beats, a dotted half note gets six beats, and a whole note gets eight beats.

The figure below shows a time signature of 3/4. That means there are three beats to the measure and the quarter note gets one beat. Thus, the three Cs in the first measure each get a single beat, marked 1, 2, 3. The second measure shows a half note C. It gets two beats (counted 1 and 2 and). It is followed by a quarter note C, which gets one beat, thus filling out the measure.

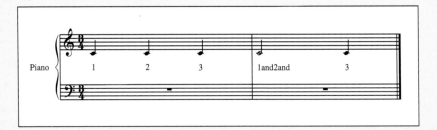

TIP

Many piano teachers encourage their beginning piano students to "count aloud." The reason for this is that actually speaking the counts (such as "one and two and . . .") out loud helps to reinforce the time signature and the note values that the student is seeing. Make it a habit to count aloud throughout this book. By the time you finish it, you will no longer need to count aloud all of the time, at least not on the familiar meters, such as 4/4 and 3/4.

Sometimes you may need to play notes that are higher or lower than on the regular staff. In printed or written piano music, these notes are accommodated by means of ledger lines and octave signs.

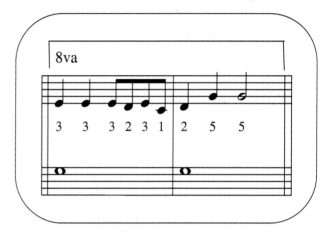

What Ledger Lines and Octave Signs Are

Ledger line notes are notes that are written on their own extra little lines above or below the staff. In "Playing 8va, 16va, and Ledger Lines," (see following page) the ledger lines are in measures 9 and 10. They show the notes high A, high B, two high Cs, then high B and high A again.

An octave sign is represented by *8va.* When you see an 8va (and a line extending along also) over the top of some treble clef notes, this tells you to play those notes an octave (that is, eight notes) *higher.* You'll learn more about the octave in Chapter 3. When 8va plus a line is written below some bass clef notes, it tells you to play those notes an octave *lower* than written. See measures 3, 4, 14, and 19 of "Playing 8va, 16va, and Ledger Lines" for examples of the 8va in the treble clef. See measures 14 and 17 for examples of the 8va in the bass clef.

16va means that you play the piece two octaves (16 notes) higher or lower than shown. This is rare, but you may see it from time to time. In "Playing 8va, 16va, and Ledger Lines," an example of 16va in the bass clef can be found in measure 19.

These two notations are helpful, because notes are easier to read on the staff than when perched well above or well below the staff.

CONTINUED ON NEXT PAGE

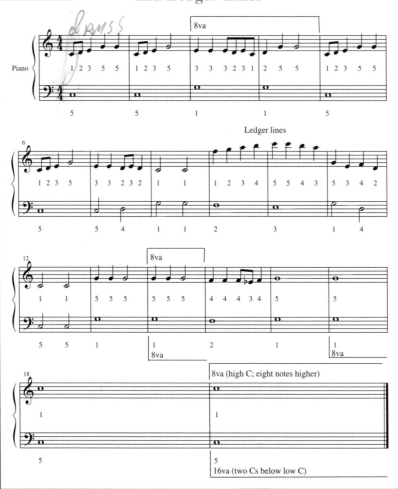

Playing 8va, 16va, and Ledger Lines

You have learned your note values, and now you can put them to use by playing a few pieces. As you play each piece, think about and begin to feel the rhythm of the note values. With practice, you will become accustomed to the note values and your playing will eventually flow naturally.

Note Value Practice Piece No. 1

In this first piece, "Note Value Piece in C," start with your thumb on C (indicated by the number 1). Place all your other fingers, as indicated (pointer = 2, middle = 3, ring = 4, and pinky = 1).

Note Value Piece in C

CONTINUED ON NEXT PAGE

Some Exercises
(continued)

Try the second piece, "Note Value Piece in F," starting with your thumb on F (instead of C), and remember to flat all your Bs. On your right hand, B♭ is played with your fourth finger; with your left hand, B♭ is played with your second finger.

Note Value Piece in F

Note Value Practice Piece No. 3

Play the third piece, "Note Value Piece in G," starting with your thumb on G, remembering that all Fs are sharp. With your right hand, when your fingers are positioned with your thumb on G, in order to play an F♯, you must cross your second finger over your thumb. Practice it a little, and it'll begin to come naturally. Chapter 6 tells you more about crossing your fingers over and under.

Note Value Piece in G

How to Practice Your Fingering

You need to practice your fingering in order to improve the strength in your fingers.

General Fingering

When practicing your fingering, it is very important to use the exact fingering notated in each piece. The circled numbers in some of this section's exercises indicate crossing over or under to reposition a finger. When a circled number appears, you have to stretch a little farther to do the cross over and under fingering. The "C Fingering Exercise" that follows gives you more practice on crossovers.

TIP

Your fourth finger is not as strong as your other fingers. Try this little exercise to understand the fourth finger's weakness. Place your hand on a flat surface, and then raise each finger as high as you can. All fingers move readily except the fourth. The fourth finger and the little finger seem to be joined together. They move easier when moving up and down at the same time, but even so, the fourth is weaker.

Now, if you were a concert pianist who practiced eight hours a day, your fourth finger would be stronger and more independent of the other fingers. Practicing the piano a lot and doing your finger exercises helps your fingers become more agile.

C Fingering Exercise

Start with the C scale, because it has no sharps or flats. (For more information on scales, see Chapter 9.) The scale covers eight notes, but because we only have five fingers, it is necessary to cross over or under the thumb and the third finger at a given time in order to have enough fingers to cover the eight-note scale. Your first cross fingering in the right hand occurs in measure 1 when your thumb crosses under your third finger. Your second cross fingering in the right hand occurs in measure 4 when your third finger crosses over your thumb. In the left hand, you'll cross your third finger over your thumb in measure 2, and your thumb under your third finger in measure 3.

CONTINUED ON NEXT PAGE

G Fingering Exercise

In playing the G scale you will sharp all Fs. As you did with the C scale, watch the fingering and use only the fingering indicated.

F Fingering Exercise

When you play the F scale, you flat all the Bs. In measures 3 and 8, your fourth finger on your right hand crosses over your thumb, and your thumb has to stretch farther when it crosses under the fourth finger in measures 2 and 7. Watch this particular fingering in this piece.

F Fingering Scale

CONTINUED ON NEXT PAGE

Additional Finger Exercises

Play these exercises one hand at a time to get your hands moving separately. When you are able to do this well, add the other hand's part and slowly move both hands together. Concentrate on one measure at a time, and soon you'll be able to move your hands at a good, steady pace.

Finger Exercise in C

As you play these additional finger exercises, be sure to keep your wrists flat, but curve your fingers and lift them high for each note.

You will notice that "Another Finger Exercise in C" does not give you the fingerings for every note. That is because you need to start figuring the fingerings out logically for yourself. From this point on, we give you some fingerings for guidance, but you will gradually be weaned away from relying on fingering numbers under every note.

Another Finger Exercise in C

CONTINUED ON NEXT PAGE

When playing in the key of G, you sharp all the Fs. (Remember that the sharp symbol in the key signature tells you this.) To start, place your right thumb on G above middle C, and your left thumb on D above middle C (it's a ledger line that you'll encounter later in measure 4).

Finger Exercise in G

Here's one additional finger exercise in G, to get you comfortable sharping all those Fs. There's a bit of a joke here and on page 40. Can you guess what it is?

Another Finger Exercise in G

CONTINUED ON NEXT PAGE

In the key of F, all Bs are flatted. (The flat symbol in the key signature tells you this.) Notice, however, the B♮ in the left hand in measure 3. In measure 3, you're going to use the second finger of your left hand twice in a row for the B♭ and B♮. Remember, too, that the B♮ is good only for measure 3; in the next measure, it reverts back to B♭. Your left thumb will be on low C, and your left hand will be in the low F position (the second F below middle C). For both this and the following exercise, your right thumb is on F.

Finger Exercise in F

Try this additional finger exercise in F, getting you used to flatting all the Bs. Maintain the same finger positions you used in the previous exercise.

Another Finger Exercise in F

3

Steps and Intervals

The piano keyboard is made up of steps and intervals. Steps can be either half (moving up one key) or whole (moving up two keys). Intervals, on the other hand, can range from an interval of a second (two white keys) to an octave (eight white keys). This chapter helps you better understand these terms and gives you pieces to play to help you learn.

Steps on the Piano Keyboard

To understand a *step* on the piano, think of walking forward. To take a step is to get from one place to another. It's the same with music. A half step or whole step moves you forward to a different note. In this section, you discover half steps and whole steps, and you begin to understand why the piano is designed the way it is. The song "Half Steps" gives you a chance to play many of the half steps on a piano keyboard. Don't worry at this point about the fingering for this piece; this exercise is only to get you used to half steps on a keyboard.

Types of Steps

HALF STEPS

Half steps are the distance from one key to the very next key. For example, C to C♯ is a half step. Most half steps are from a white key to a black key or from a black key to a white key. Half steps from white key to white key are marked with an H in the photo.

WHOLE STEPS

A whole step is defined as two half steps; in other words, a whole step is the distance between two keys, with one key (black or white) in between. F to G is a whole step (with F♯ in between). D to E is also a whole step, with E♭ being the note in between. See the figure below for additional steps.

In the exercise called "Whole Steps" you play many of the whole steps on the piano keyboard. As with half steps, don't worry at all about fingering; you're only getting yourself used to playing whole steps.

CONTINUED ON NEXT PAGE

ENHARMONICS

Have you noticed that each black key has two names? The term for this is *enharmonics,* a word that points out that each black key is both a sharp and a flat. The key between G and A, for example, could be called either G♯ or A♭. As you move up the keyboard, the black key to the right of a white key is the sharp of the white key. So, the black key to the right of G is G♯. But when you move down the keyboard, the black key to the left of the white key is the flat of the white key. So the black key to the left of A is A♭. But if you look at the keyboard, you'll see that both G♯ and A♭ are the same key.

The exercise called "Enharmonics Piece" shows you how the same key on the keyboard can be called two different notes on a staff. As with the two previous pieces, the purpose is not to practice your fingering but to have you look at the enharmonics that are on your keyboard.

An *interval* is the distance between two notes. This is an important term to learn because certain intervals are preferred by certain cultures. This is especially true in ethnic music: Asian music is strongly represented in intervals of fourths; Native American music often has intervals of the fifth.

Types of Intervals

INTERVAL OF A SECOND

An interval of a second covers two white keys. For example, if you first play C and move to the very next note, D, you've played two notes, the first, and then the second. This is why musicians use the term "second" for this distance on the keyboard.

INTERVAL OF A THIRD

If you play one key, say C, and then move up two keys, E, you've covered the distance between three keys (C, D, and E), and so musicians call this interval a "third."

ADDITIONAL INTERVALS

Intervals of the fourth, fifth, sixth, and seventh degrees continue this pattern. An interval of the fourth is from C to F; an interval of a fifth is from C to G; an interval of a sixth is from C to A; an interval of a seventh is from C to B.

AN OCTAVE

As discussed in Chapter 2's section on the 8va sign, an interval of an eighth—for example, from middle C to high C—is called an octave.

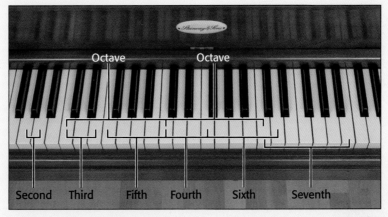

CONTINUED ON NEXT PAGE

Keyboard
Intervals *(continued)*

The song called "Intervals" shows you a variety of intervals. When you've practiced a bit, test your knowledge by naming the unnamed intervals shown in the piece. The answers are at the end of this chapter.

The exercises in this section enable you to practice what you've learned thus far.

To help you read the music, the note names are provided below the notes on the staff. As you progress through this book, the note names will not be given, so you might try covering up the note names as you scan each piece.

Before you begin playing, review the song and think about the notes before you actually play the piece. Relate the notes on the staff to keys on the keyboard, so that this process becomes second nature to you as you practice.

Don't get discouraged. Play slowly at first, speeding up as you get more comfortable.

"PLAYING RIGHT-HAND NOTE NAMES"

In this piece you play just a handful of notes. Slowly play a measure at a time, and then play two measures at a time. Continually add more measures as you go. Then go back and play from beginning to end.

CONTINUED ON NEXT PAGE

"BLUESY"

To play "Bluesy," first check the key signature and make sure you know which three notes are flatted throughout the piece. This piece was written to show you how something sounds when it is written in a minor mood (later, we'll say it is in a minor key—see Chapter 9). In this case, the mood is somber, like the blues. Watch carefully to play all the flatted and sharped notes, because they play a great role in creating the minor mood.

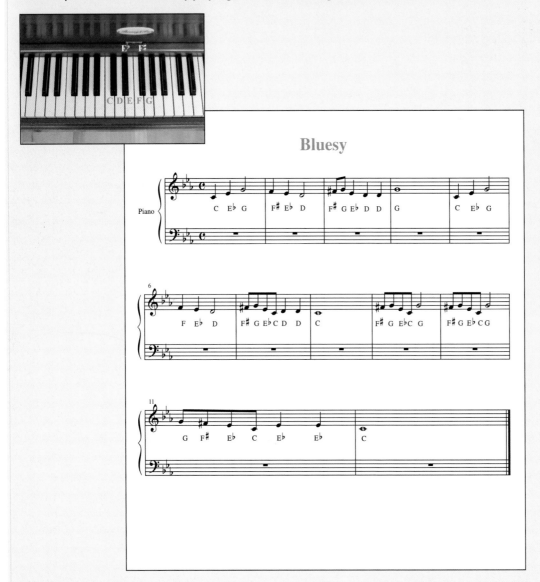

"A SONG FOR LEFTY MIDDLE C"

The next few songs, of which "A Song for Lefty Middle C" is the first, are intended to give your left hand a good exercise in playing by itself. Note the time signature (see Chapter 2), which is in 3/4. Don't rush this piece; let your left hand flow slowly.

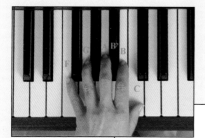

A Song for Lefty Middle C

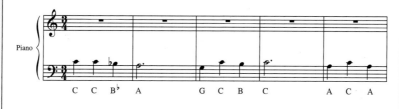

C C B♭ A   G C B C   A C A

G A C B   B A B C C B♭ A   B B G

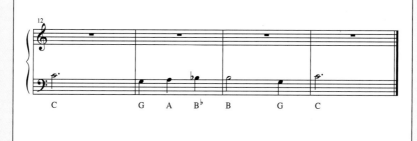

C   G A B♭ B   G C

CONTINUED ON NEXT PAGE

"LEFTY C JAZZ"

This piece gives you another opportunity to exercise the left hand as a solo part. Usually the left hand is the accompanying part, but "Lefty C Jazz" allows your left hand to sing out a melody.

"LEFTY PLAYS THE LOW C POSITION"

This left-hand piece uses many eighth notes. This left-hand style is used in rock 'n' roll, jazz, boogie woogie, and other types of music (discussed in more detail in Chapter 10). It has to be played very slowly at first, because your left hand will play a lot of notes in each measure.

The low C position for the left hand starts your pinky on low C. Arrange your other left-hand fingers so that they move up the keyboard (fourth on D, third on E, second on F, and first on G).

CONTINUED ON NEXT PAGE

"SAD LEFTY LOW"

Play "Sad Lefty Low" very slowly, because of the tempo marking of lento (which is discussed further in Chapter 4). Note the mood of sadness, which comes from this piece's minor key of C (see Chapter 9 for more on minor keys), where the notes of B, E, and A are flatted.

Sad Lefty Low

"MINUET"

"Minuet," based on a piece by Johann Sebastian Bach, moves back and forth between the left and right hands. Start your left hand in middle C position, with your thumb on middle C. Watch for exact fingering and practice a little at a time. This piece should have a light and airy feel. Don't try to play it too fast.

Arpeggios

The word *arpeggio* is Italian for "in the style of a harp." The main purpose of this exercise is to become comfortable playing notes that are separated from one another on the keyboard. For more about arpeggios, see "Solid and Broken Chords" in Chapter 6.

The practice drill included for you ("Arpeggio Exercise") is a pattern within an octave, starting on the bottom note of the octave with your thumb, playing some of the notes of the octave with your middle three fingers, and moving up to the top part of the octave with your fifth finger. The notes used in the first measure of this ascending pattern are C, E, G, and high C. Coming down in the second measure, the notes used are high C, G, E, and middle C.

The next measure starts on E and moves up to the top of the E octave, and then comes down in the following measure, and so on.

These arpeggios cover more notes than you're used to at this point, and if you have small hands, it may take a little extra practice to stretch your fingers to reach the notes. Keep doing this exercise until you feel comfortable with the reach.

Start out with a measure at a time. Look at each starting note in each measure and follow the notation.

Study your keyboard pictures on page 60 that show different positions of notes and fingerings for C, G, and F.

TIP

Play arpeggios very slowly at the beginning, using only the fingering shown. Like all drills and exercises, you want to play this piece over and over (and over and over) until you can play it in your sleep. Speed up your play as you become more comfortable with the exercise.

Arpeggio Exercise

CONTINUED ON NEXT PAGE

C ARPEGGIOS AND INVERSIONS

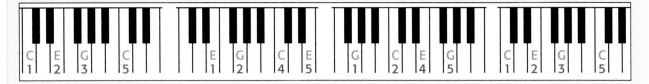

G ARPEGGIOS AND INVERSIONS

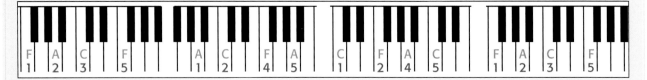

F ARPEGGIOS AND INVERSIONS

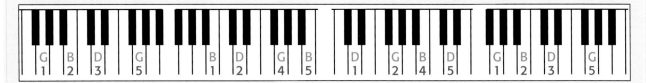

Here are the answers to the test you took at the end of the "Intervals" exercise on page 50.

Answers to Intervals Test				
Measure No.	**1st note**	**2nd note**	**3rd note**	**4th note**
10	third	third	fourth	fourth
11	fifth	third	fourth	second
12	sixth	fifth	fourth	third
13	third	sixth	fifth	octave
14	fifth	fifth	sixth	third
15	second	third	fourth	fifth
16	sixth	fourth	seventh	fifth
17	octave			

4

Dynamics and Tempo

To breathe life into your piano playing, you can vary both your loudness or softness (dynamics) and speed and energy (tempo). Both dynamics and tempo change the expressiveness of your pieces—without varying these two qualities, your music will likely seem uninteresting to those listening.

Italian words are used to specify both the dynamics and tempo of a piece, so dust off your best Italian accent and get ready to add a few terms to your vocabulary.

Dynamics

Dynamics pertains to the loudness and softness of the music you're playing, as marked on the piano music itself. For difficult pieces, the dynamics can become more complex, even perhaps changing every measure or two (and you'll see some of these in this chapter to get you used to changing your dynamics midway through a song). But some simple pieces specify the dynamics only at the beginning of the piece, and you maintain that loudness or softness throughout.

The symbols in the first column below are commonly found in piano music. They stand for Italian words that identify dynamic levels. One of the benefits of learning to play the piano is that you learn some Italian as well!

pp	pianissimo	very soft
p	piano	soft
mp	mezzo piano	moderately soft
mf	mezzo forte	moderately loud
f	forte	loud
ff	fortissimo	very loud

Dynamics can also indicate a change in loudness or softness. These changes are also expressed by Italian words. *Crescendo* means getting louder and is marked with a long < that opens (to indicate getting louder) as it gets to the end. The reverse of this is *decrescendo,* which means getting softer, and is marked with a long >, indicating graphically that the sound begins to get softer. These two marks may remind you of the less-than and greater-than signs you learned in your middle school math classes. Another term, *sforzando,* written as *sfz,* means suddenly loud or with strong accent.

The exercise called "Sentimental" gives you a chance to try out some dynamics, specifically *p, mp, mf,* and *p.* Start in the hand positions shown.

Sentimental

CONTINUED ON NEXT PAGE

"Happy Time" lets you try gradually changing the loudness. Start off playing a crescendo softly, and gradually increase until you are playing quite loudly at the end of the crescendo. Do the opposite for a decrescendo. Put your right and left thumbs on middle C, and play according to the finger placement shown.

"SFZ Tune" helps you practice the sudden loudness of *sforzando.* Note that the hand positions are like those used in "Sentimental."

A *tie* is shown by a line connecting two notes of the same pitch. You play the first note and hold it to its correct time value. You do *not* play the second note; instead, you keep holding the first note for the number of beats indicated by the second note's time value.

"Tie You Down" helps you practice playing ties. Just remember to hold the tie for the entire length shown by the two tied notes.

Tie You Down

Syncopation

Although being off-beat is usually not a good thing in music, when you play with *syncopation*, you play notes just before or just after a beat, or you stress a beat that normally isn't stressed. For example, in a waltz, which is in 3/4 time, the first beat is usually stressed—ONE, two, three, ONE, two, three, ONE, two, three. A waltz with syncopation might sound more like ONE, two, THREE or one, TWO, three. Syncopation is heard most in ragtime, jazz, and Latin music.

In "Syncopate a Dance," you get to practice a syncopated rhythm. Here, the syncopation is provided by the tied eighth notes. Before playing, tap out the rhythm, and then slowly play the piece.

Syncopate a Dance

A *phrase* is a group of notes expressing an idea. The idea is to play all the notes in that group (or phrase) in a smooth manner.

A phrase of music expresses a complete thought, just as a sentence in English (or another language) expresses a complete thought. At the end of the sentence is a period. Think of a phrase as a complete sentence; you connect the notes in a complete thought.

Practice "Phrases in Song" and play each of the three phrases that are complete in and of themselves: The first phrase is measures 1, 2, 3, and 4; the second phrase encompasses measures 5, 6, 7, and 8; and the third phrase includes measures 9, 10, 11, and 12.

Phrases in Song

Tempo

Tempo is a word that musicians use in regard to how fast to play. You don't want to try to play fast at first, while you are still in the early stages of learning piano, but as you progress, you'll be able to master the correct tempos.

Tempo Markings in Music

Tempo markings indicate the rate of speed at which you should play a musical composition. Like dynamic markings, tempo markings are often in Italian. The most common tempo markings are as follows:

largo	very slow
lento	at a much slower rate
adagio	still meaning slowly
andante	moving pace or walking tempo
andantino	a little faster
moderato	moderate speed
allegretto	quick pace
allegro	lively
vivace	quickly (equals or exceeds allegro)
presto	very fast
prestissimo	faster than presto

You have to approximate what's meant by "very slow" or "lively," but you'll get a better sense of this, the more you play.

Two exercises help you practice tempo. The first, "Sad Song," is played largo, very slowly. The second, "Run, Run, Run," however, is played vivace—quickly—although you may need to practice this piece several times before you can get it to that quick pace.

Sad Song

CONTINUED ON NEXT PAGE

Run, Run, Run

Using a Metronome

The *metronome* is a valuable little instrument that helps you keep a steady tempo. They aren't cheap, but a good metronome will last you the rest of your life.

A marking at the beginning of a musical composition dictates how to adjust your metronome. The marking is preceded by M.M., and numbers on the metronome correlate to this number.

Think of your metronome as a conductor with a baton who is keeping the tempo steady. You'll find that you need it less and less, but at the very least, it gets you started with the correct tempo.

FAQ

The metronome shown on this page is the classic (some would say old-fashioned) kind that mechanically counts beats by moving from side to side. You can also purchase an electronic metronome, which is a higher-tech version.

CONTINUED ON NEXT PAGE

"Ballgame" gives you a great practice piece on which to see how your metronome works. Here, a quarter note is equal to 150. Note that you start with both thumbs on middle C.

Ballgame

Patterns

In a *pattern* or *sequence* of notes, you repeat the rhythm and/or direction of the notes, but you use different notes. So, the first measure may begin a pattern with C, D, E, C. The same pattern but with different notes might be D, F, G, D or F, G, A, F.

Note the patterns in "Patterns in a Song." This piece gives you two patterns to recognize and practice.

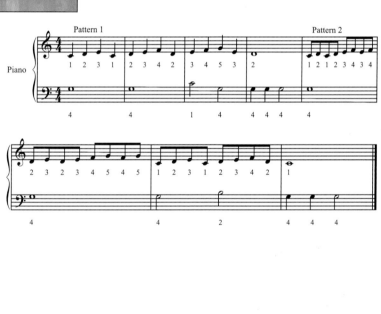

Patterns in a Song

chapter **5**

Warming Up

Warming up is critical to successfully mastering the piano. Getting your hands and fingers loose and pliable enables you to play challenging pieces with ease. This chapter shows you how to warm up with both hands. You also get some practice, for the first time, in playing pieces that do not give finger numbers or note names.

Right-Hand Five-Finger Warm Ups with Numbers

This exercise gets your right-hand fingers moving. Start with your right thumb on middle C, with your fingers curved. Now play the warm-up exercise, which is labeled with numbers instead of note names.

Keep in mind that fast is not always better. Instead, play slowly at first to improve your technique. Think of the steady ticking of a clock—that's what you're striving for.

Left-Hand Five-Finger Warm Ups with Numbers

You'll warm up at both middle C and low C in the left hand.

Keep in mind that your left hand tends to be weaker than your right hand. Don't get discouraged by this, though. Strength in your left hand will come with concentrated practice. Just as in playing tennis or golf, be patient and give your finger muscles time to strengthen.

Middle C

Place your left thumb on middle C and follow the numbered finger markings. As you did with the right hand exercise, play the notes slowly and with good pressure from your fingers.

Left-Hand Middle C
Warm Up with Numbers

CONTINUED ON NEXT PAGE

Low C

Place your little finger on low C, one octave down from middle C. This is where your left hand will most often be positioned when you play the piano, because the left hand functions mostly as an accompaniment to the right hand.

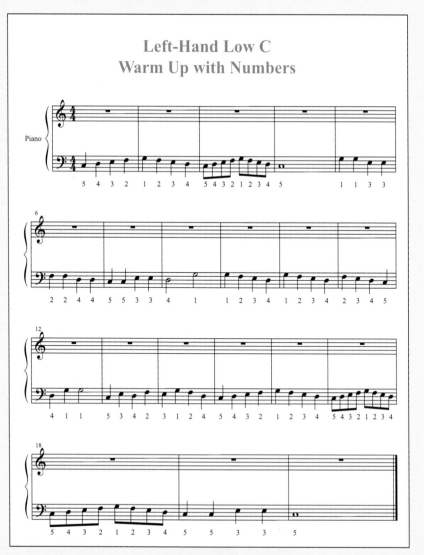

Printed music that you buy and play on the piano doesn't show finger numbering; it shows only the notes on a staff (see Chapter 2). Eventually, you'll be able to read notes on a staff without any assistance. For now, we've replaced finger numbers with note names.

As you play each note, say its name and concentrate on its location on the keyboard. Also think about how it looks on the staff. Keep the note values in mind. As a reminder: The black note heads with a stem are quarter notes, and they get one count each. The white note heads are half notes, and they get two counts each. Groups of black note heads with connected bar-like stems are called eighth notes, and each group of *two* gets one count. One eighth note by itself, which has a little flag on it, gets only half a count. Now place your right thumb on middle C and proceed to do the exercise.

Right-Hand Warm Up with Note Names

Left-Hand Five-Finger Warm Ups with Note Names

As before, with your left hand, you'll warm up at both middle C and low C. These exercises, however, no longer show finger numbers; they show only note names.

Middle C

Place your left thumb on middle C. In this exercise, you will practice learning your five notes by their names. Your thumb is at middle C, your second finger is on B. Your third finger is on A. Your fourth finger is on G. Your pinky is on F.

As you play the warm-up drill, say the note names and look at the staff to remember how the notes look on the lines and spaces.

Left-Hand Middle C
Warm Up with Note Names

Low C

Place your little finger on low C. Proceed up the five-finger pattern by putting your fourth finger on D, your third finger on E, your second finger on F, and your thumb on G.

Left-Hand Low C Warm Up with Note Names

Now it is time to play a solo with your right hand. You will be playing melodies like this one with your right hand most of the time, while your left hand will supply accompaniment using single notes or chords (see Chapter 6).

Try to play this solo, called "Just for You," with feeling. Enjoy your performance!

Just for You

The two exercises in this section encourage you to play both hands together. For both pieces, the right hand shows only note names (not finger numbering), while the left hand shows finger numbers. Many of the notes aren't labeled at all, in an attempt to get you reading music without any help.

"A MINUET"

Place both thumbs on middle C, and remember that your fingers will take turns as you play this piece. Simply lift one thumb up while the other needs to play.

Practice each hand separately at first. After playing with each hand apart, slowly play with both hands together.

A Minuet

CONTINUED ON NEXT PAGE

"BILL BAILEY"

To start, place your right thumb on middle C and your left pinky on low C. In "Bill Bailey," you sometimes use both hands at the same time.

Bill Bailey

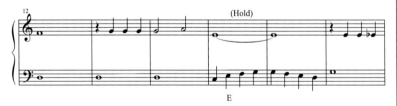

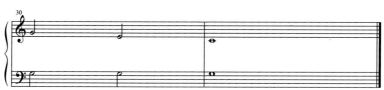

Playing without Finger Numbers or Note Names

You're now ready to play a piece that shows you neither finger numbering nor note names (except at the very beginning). Before starting, always check the key signature and time signature, and look through the piece to see if there are any accidentals (sharps or flats)—see Chapter 2 for more on these.

Play the "F Position Warm Up" before beginning. Also look at the keyboard photo for your proper starting hand position. You're then ready to begin the piece called "Let's Have Fun Playing the Piano." Just make sure you do have fun!

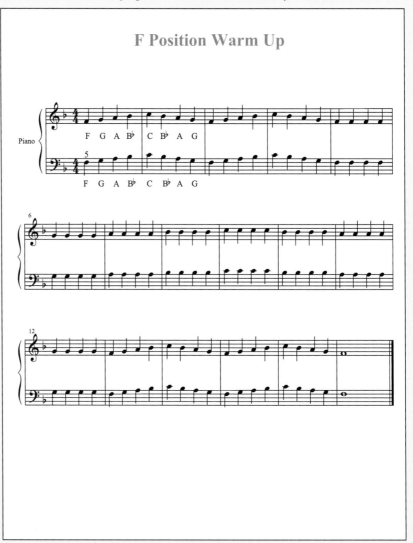

F Position Warm Up

Let's Have Fun Playing the Piano

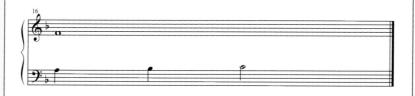

chapter 6

Chords

Chords are three, four, or five notes played at the same time. In this chapter, you will learn three basic chords—C, F, and G—and play several pieces to help you recognize these chords by sight. You also will discover the difference between solid and broken chords.

A chord is built on the interval of a third, which is a combination of three notes (see Chapter 3 for details).

To play a C chord with your left hand, place your fifth finger on low C, and your third finger on E. Playing these two keys together gives you the interval of a third that makes up the bottom part of the C chord.

To add the last note (the interval of a fifth)—and, therefore, play the entire C chord—place the thumb of your left hand on G (see photo on next page). You've done it: You just played a C chord.

A three-note chord is called a *triad,* which means three. The bottom note is the *root* of the chord, and the chord gets its name from the name of the root.

Now play the C chord exercise. Watch your rhythm, remembering to give correct time values to the notes/chords, as discussed in Chapter 2. Remember, a whole note equals four counts, a half note equals two counts, and a quarter note equals one count.

C Chord Exercise

CONTINUED ON NEXT PAGE

Now that you have played your C chord exercise, here are two songs that will help you practice C chords: "A Song in C" and "Play with a Chord."

A Song in C

Play with a Chord

F Chord

To play the F chord, place your left pinky on F, below middle C. You will build the F chord in the same way you built the C chord—by playing the root, third, and fifth of the F chord. This time, your fifth finger is F (the root), your third finger is on A (the third), and your thumb is on middle C (the fifth).

Play the F chord drill just as you did in the C chord exercise, noting that the B is flatted. Then practice more F chords in "A Song in F."

A Song in F

G Chord

To play a G chord, place your left-hand pinky on G, below middle C. The root (fifth finger) is G, and your third finger is on B. Your thumb is on the D above middle C.

Play your exercise for learning chords in G, and then proceed to play "Playing a Piece in G." The sharp at the beginning where the key signature appears is F. As you know from Chapter 2, this means that if there are any Fs in the piece, they are all sharped, unless a natural sign appears.

Chords in G

Playing a Piece in G

Solid and Broken Chords

In many piano pieces, the main purpose of the left hand is to provide the harmony and rhythmic accompaniment. This allows you to have the fun of producing great melodies with your right hand.

You've been playing *solid chords,* in which the notes are stacked on top of each other on the staff, and your hand plays all the notes at the same time. "Playing with Solid Chords" gives you another opportunity to play solid chords.

Playing with Solid Chords

When a chord is *broken,* the notes in the chord are separated. This gives the chord a sense of movement, and allows variety and rhythm in a piece. An *arpeggio* (discussed in Chapter 3), is essentially a broken chord—you're simply playing one note of the chord at a time.

Notice the broken chords in the exercise titled "Playing with Broken Chords." Start with a slow but steady tempo and play the left hand alone. The broken chords need to flow as smoothly as possible before you put your right hand with your left.

While playing this piece, you'll begin to feel the even movement of the three-note pattern in the left hand.

Playing with Broken Chords

Crossing Fingers Over and Under

A special technique can help you move your fingers up the keyboard without getting all twisted up, especially when playing broken chords.

With this technique, you move your fingers over or under each other. Sometimes your forefinger needs to cross over your thumb, and sometimes the notes will require your thumb to move under your forefinger.

The Technique

Here's how to practice: Play an F with your right thumb and then play an E with your second finger. Now play a C but instead of using your third finger, use your thumb. Notice how your thumb crosses under your forefinger.

Now place your thumb on G and play an E with your second finger. Note that your forefinger is crossing over your thumb.

Practice crossing over and under on the song called "Finger Over and Under." First, warm up with a scale, and then play the more difficult piece.

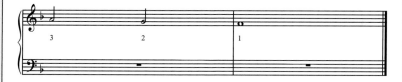

F Scale Warm Up

CONTINUED ON NEXT PAGE

Practice "Fingers Over and Under" using the fingering hints supplied to you in the music.

Fingers Over and Under

CONTINUED ON NEXT PAGE

For additional practice with chords, play these pieces, which are a bit more advanced than the exercises you've already seen in this chapter. Each "Dream On" piece includes a warm-up exercise to help get your fingers moving.

Chord Practice Pieces

"DREAM ON IN MOSTLY C"

In "Dream On in Mostly C," notice how the melody remains in the right hand, which is very common.

Play the warm up first, and then proceed to this piece. Practice with your hands apart, and then slowly put them together after you've learned each hand well.

As you play, watch for all the key signature markings, as well as tempo and dynamic markings, and the position of your hands.

Warm Ups in C

CONTINUED ON NEXT PAGE

Dream On in Mostly C

"DREAM ON IN F"

When you play the same piece in F, notice how the melody switches back and forth from the left hand to the right hand. When this occurs, the non-melody hand is playing the harmony and accompaniment.

Before playing your piece, remember to do the warm-up exercise. Then practice the piece with your hands apart before putting both hands together.

CONTINUED ON NEXT PAGE

"DREAM ON IN G"

Play "Dream On" again, now in another key and position, after doing the warm up.

Be sure and look carefully at your hand positions. Your right hand will be in the familiar middle C position, with your right thumb on middle C. Your left hand will learn the new position in the key of G: Put your left thumb on D above middle C, and your left pinky on G, below middle C (as shown in the keyboard photo below).

CONTINUED ON NEXT PAGE

Dream On in G

By now, you have played chords and know that a chord is made up of three notes: a root, a third, and a fifth.

When you play an *inversion* (or "invert the chord"), you still play the notes that comprise the root, the third, and the fifth in the chord, but you put them in different positions—essentially, turning them around. You still play the same three notes, but you play some of them one octave down or up from where you would with a standard chord.

It is sometimes hard to move from chord to chord; In many cases, it's much easier to invert the position of the notes in the chord. An inversion is a good way to create different sounds and enable the pianist to move quickly from one chord to another. See the accompanying figures for inversions in the keys of C, G, and F.

TIP

In order to learn how to play chords in different positions, you have to become comfortable with the *feel* of the chords. Not only do you have to get used to seeing how a chord looks on the page and hearing how it sounds, but you also need to experience how it feels to have your hands in that chord's position. With practice, your hands will "remember" the chord position in the future.

As you practice, move from one inversion to another, and then back again to the first, over and over. Move back and forth, back and forth until you get a feel for each position.

CONTINUED ON NEXT PAGE

Inversions in C

Root position (C on bottom)

1st inversion (E on bottom)

2nd inversion (G on bottom)

Root position (C on bottom)

Inversions in G

Root position (G on bottom)

1st inversion (B on bottom)

2nd inversion (D on bottom)

Root position (G on bottom)

CONTINUED ON NEXT PAGE

Inversions in F

Root position (F on bottom)

1st inversion (A on bottom)

2nd inversion (C on bottom)

Root position (F on bottom)

The piece "Inversions for the Left Hand in C, G, and F" lets you try inversions in all three keys. Note that the piece shows only the left hand, because the left hand usually plays the accompaniment, which is often made up of chords and their inversions.

In this piece, you're going to change hand positions twice as the key changes. Use the photos on the following page to position your hands for each key change.

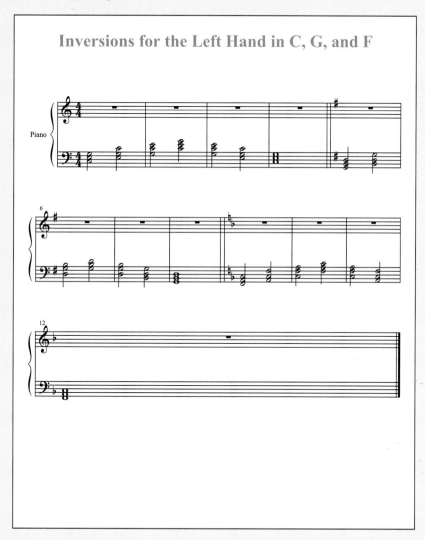

CONTINUED ON NEXT PAGE

C chord position for inversions

G chord position for inversions

F chord position for inversions

Now play these three different pieces: "Inversions in C," "Inversions in G," and "Inversions in F."

In "Inversions in G," note the A and D chords in measures 7 and 8, respectively. These are new inversions you haven't seen before, but they often occur when playing in the key of G.

Inversions in C

CONTINUED ON NEXT PAGE

Inversions in G

Inversions in F

Lead Sheets

A *lead sheet* is a piece of music that displays only the right-hand portion—that is, the melody. Instead of showing the staff, with both bass and treble clef (see Chapter 2), a lead sheet shows only the upper set of the staff. Above the notes for the right-hand melody, you see note names (called *chord symbols)* that explain which notes are to be played in the left-hand chord.

Writing music this way is shorthand for the composer/arranger, and it allows the musician to be more flexible in how the left-hand chords are played. All you know is the chord to play, but not whether to play a standard chord or an inversion. You can eventually begin to learn how to create the left-hand treatment in a way that sounds good to you.

Go ahead and play the piece entitled "Lead Sheet Example." First play the right-hand melody line and become familiar with it. Then play the left hand alone and work on the chords. When you see a chord symbol written above a measure, play the chord or an inversion of the chord until the chord symbol changes.

The photos on the next page give you visual aids for finding the G, F, D, and C chords. The dots represent where you place your hands.

Lead Sheet Example

G chord

F chord

D chord

C chord

CONTINUED ON NEXT PAGE

Now you can play more complex pieces in C, G, and F using lead sheets. Start by playing "Lead Sheet in C."

The photos on the following page help you find the C, F, and G chords, as well as where to place your right hand. The numbers in these photos tell you where to place your fingers.

Lead Sheet in C

Right hand

C chord

F chord

G chord

CONTINUED ON NEXT PAGE

Finally, try playing off a lead sheet that uses chord inversions. When playing from a lead sheet and you see a chord followed by a slash, the next note is the one that should be on the bottom. So, the notation G/B means that B should be on the bottom (first inversion).

Be sure to use the photos on the next page to help you place your fingers.

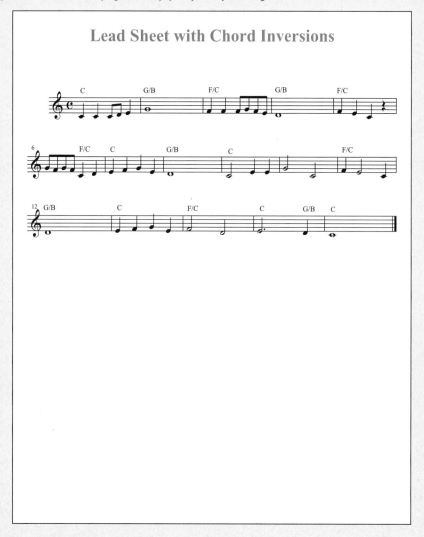

Lead Sheet with Chord Inversions

C chord (root position)

G/B chord (B on bottom)

F/C chord (C on bottom)

CONTINUED ON NEXT PAGE

"Lead Sheet in G" gives you another chance to use a lead sheet, but this time, you're playing in G. Use the photos on the next page to help you place your fingers.

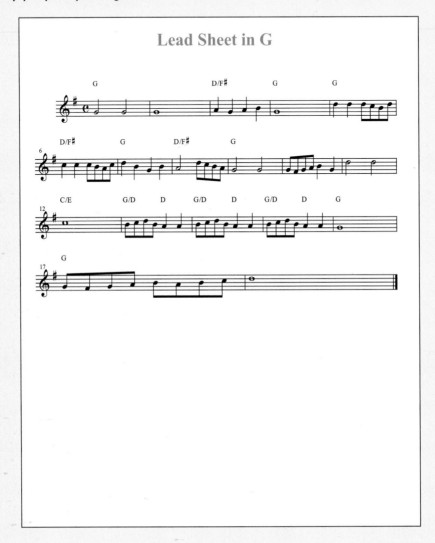

Lead Sheet in G

G chord

D/F♯ chord

C/E chord

G/D chord

D chord

CONTINUED ON NEXT PAGE

Lead Sheets
(continued)

Finally, here's a lead sheet exercise in the key of F. Use the photos on the next page to help you place your fingers.

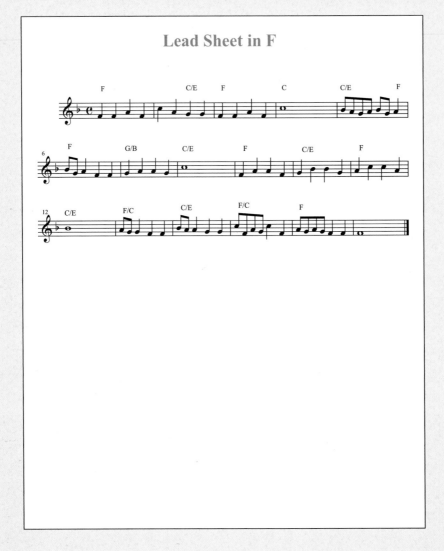

Right hand

F chord

C/E chord

F/C chord

G/B chord

Three Jazz Pieces to Practice Chords

To practice the chords you've learned in this chapter, play these three fun jazz pieces. As with any challenging piece, practice each hand separately until you master them, and then put both hands together.

To find out a bit more about jazz, see Chapter 10.

Jazz Piece #1

CONTINUED ON NEXT PAGE

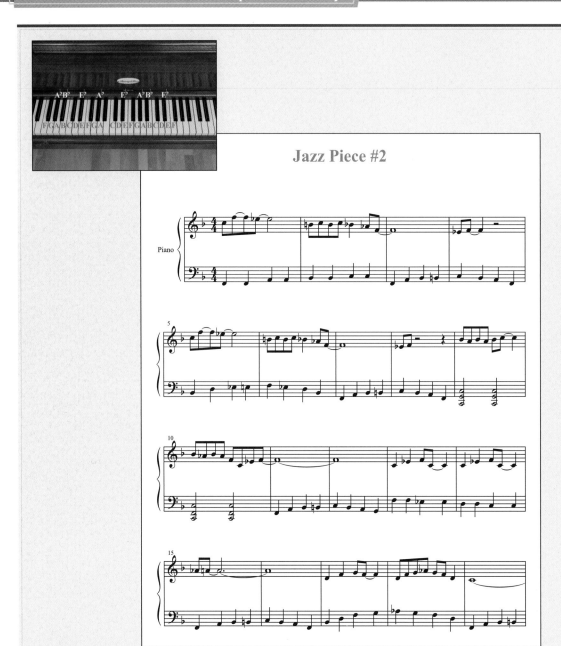

Jazz Piece #2

CONTINUED ON NEXT PAGE

This piece has only a few chords to practice, but we've included it to help you practice playing a melody with your left hand. Although the left hand most often plays chords or single notes, in this piece—as with much of jazz music—the left hand is far more active.

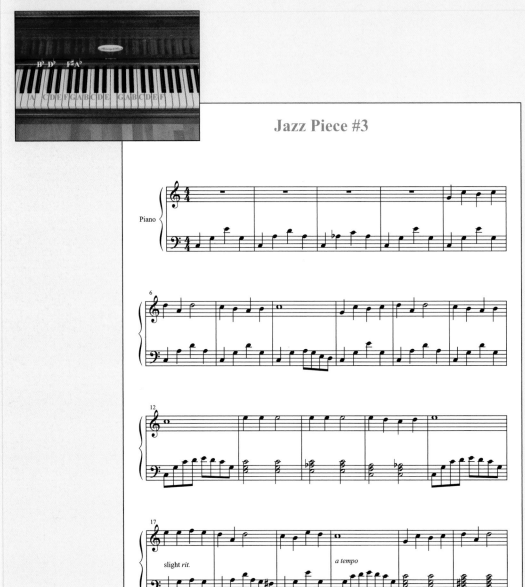

Jazz Piece #3

chapter 7

Meter, Harmony, and Movement

In this chapter, you build on the lesson on time signatures in Chapter 2 and learn advanced ways to play piano meters (a *meter* is how measures are divided into a certain number of beats; 4/4 is a meter, as is 3/4), namely upbeats and waltz time. You also will get some practice in sight reading (sitting down to play a piece you haven't seen before) and discover four-part harmony—just like a barbershop quartet, but on a piano.

Playing in Waltz Time

A waltz is a type of music that originally was associated with a specific kind of dance. This dance first became popular many years ago at British and French social gatherings. Some famous waltzes include the "Tennessee Waltz," "Let Me Call You Sweetheart," and "Moon River." When playing in *waltz time,* you're playing three beats to a measure. The time signature (see Chapter 2) indicates whether a piece is in waltz time, which is usually 3/4 meter. In 3/4 meter, the song gets three counts (beats) to a measure, and every quarter note gets one count. In 6/8 meter, a variation on waltz time, every eighth note gets one count, and the song has six counts to a measure.

Since you learned how to play chords in Chapter 6, the first waltz presented here is "Left-Hand Waltz Solid Chords." Practice this exercise with each hand separately first, then proceed slowly with your hands together.

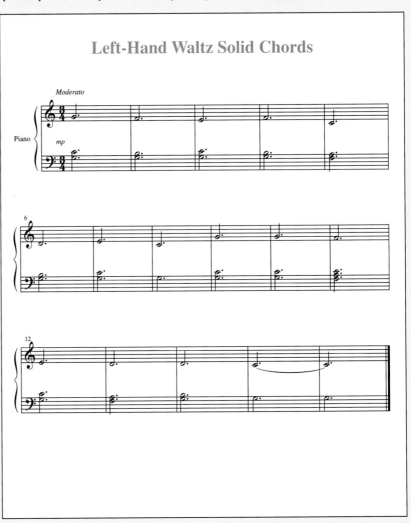

Left-Hand Waltz Solid Chords

1.0

To add movement to your left hand while playing a waltz, you can play broken chords (see Chapter 6). "Playing Waltz Time with Broken Chords," below, has the same notes that you encountered in "Left-Hand Waltz Solid Chords," but now the notes of the chords are played separately.

Playing Waltz Time with Broken Chords

The term *sight reading* refers to an exercise in which you play something you haven't seen before. The purpose of sight reading is to test yourself on how well you play a piece the first time you see it. This helps you become a better reader in the future. Each time you sight read, your ability to read music improves.

This exercise in sight-reading displays chords (see Chapter 6 for details on chords) that you'll also see in many hymns and classical music pieces. Looking at these four-chord notes, all at one time, is a great test of your ability to sight read.

Practice this sight-reading piece. First work on the part written in the C position (measures 1–4), with your right hand on middle C, and your left hand in the low C position. Then follow the same procedure in the key of G (measures 5–8), with your right thumb on G, and your left thumb on the D above middle C. The sharp in the key signature tells you that all Fs are sharp.

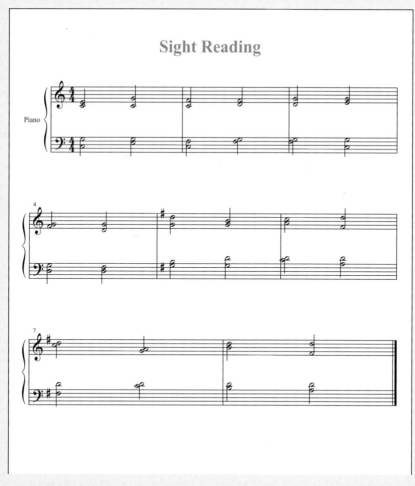

Sight Reading

C position

G position

Playing Four-Part Harmony

Four-part harmony is found in choirs, in which you have four different voices, ranging from high to low. The soprano voice is the highest, the alto voice is slightly lower, the tenor voice is lower still, and the bass is the lowest. A barbershop quartet is, perhaps, the best-known example of four-part harmony. Many hymns are also written in four-part harmony.

In "Four-Part Harmony in C, G, and F," your right hand plays two notes, while your left hand plays the other two notes. Be forewarned that you will reposition your hands two times during this piece (see the following page).

Four-Part Harmony in C, G, and F

C position

G position

F position

Parallel Motion

Parallel motion means that both your hands are moving in the same direction, such that both your hands are going up the scale (or down) at the same time.

Play all of the following exercises in parallel motion. "Exercise in Parallel Motion" begins in the C position, moves to G position, and then finally moves to F position. Look at each hand position on the following page before you start.
Note: At the end of lines 1 and 2 (after measures 5 and 10, respectively), you see key signature changes. No, there is no music missing there. The sharps and flats you see are there to alert you that there will be a key signature change on the next line (measures 6 and 11, respectively).

Exercise in Parallel Motion

C position

G position

F position

CONTINUED ON NEXT PAGE

Playing a Piece in Parallel Motion

Playing a Piece in Parallel G

Piano

CONTINUED ON NEXT PAGE

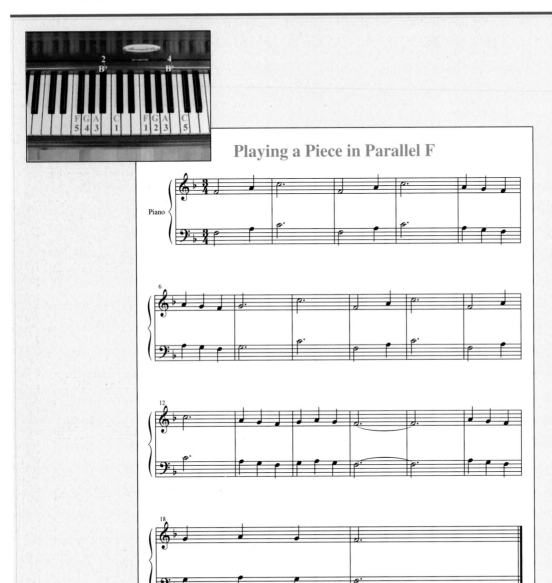

Playing a Piece in Parallel F

An *upbeat* is a note (or notes) that appears before the first complete measure. When you add the incomplete count of the upbeat measure to the incomplete count of beats in the last measure, you have the correct number of counts needed in a measure.

Look at the piece called "Are You Upbeat?" to see how upbeats work. This piece is in 4/4 time, but notice that the first measure shows three quarter notes leading into the first complete measure, which has a whole note. Look at the last measure and see how the count is only one quarter note.

At the end of the piece, do what's called a *turnaround*—meaning that when you get to the last measure, play the one-count quarter note, then immediately go back to the first measure and pick up the remaining three counts, then continue with the music. Perform this turnaround the first time you go through the piece; then stop at the end of the piece after you have played it a second time through. Although we haven't shown any in "Are You Upbeat?," in Chapter 8, you'll learn how to read signs in piano music that tell you how to repeat certain sections of music.

Give this piece a whirl!

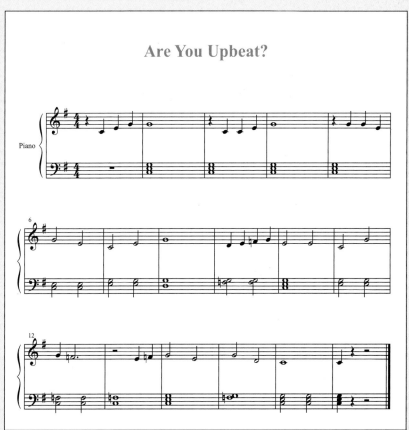

Are You Upbeat?

Contrary Motion

When you play in *contrary motion*, your hands move in opposite directions, with one hand going up the scale, while the other goes down.

Play "Contrary Motion Exercise in C," keeping in mind that the purpose of the exercise is to encourage steady movement. Then play "A Piece in C Contrary."

Next, play "Contrary Motion Exercise in G," and then play "A Piece in G Contrary."

Finally, play "Contrary Motion Exercise in F," and then move on to "A Piece in F Contrary."

As needed, look at the photos that accompany each piece for your proper hand positions.

A Piece in C Contrary

CONTINUED ON NEXT PAGE

Contrary Motion Exercise in G

A Piece in G Contrary

CONTINUED ON NEXT PAGE

Contrary Motion Exercise in F

A Piece in F Contrary

Advanced Musical Terms

Pieces written for the piano include all sorts of notations—both written words and symbols—so that you play the piece as the composer or arranger intended. Most of those notations are Italian words or have Italian names, so you may need a bit of help in translating them. This chapter helps you read all of these challenging notations, from *staccato* and *legato* to *D.C. al Fine, ritardando,* and *decrescendo.*

Staccato and Legato

Two terms, staccato and legato, dictate how you strike the keys with your fingers. One is short and crisp, while the other is smooth.

STACCATO

Staccato describes one of the ways you can play a note; in this case, like you've touched a hot iron. You strike the key, and then quickly lift your finger off the key, so that the note you play is choppy and light.

When you see a dot *over* or *under* a note, that note is to be played staccato.

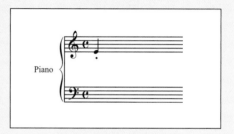

LEGATO

Legato means smooth and connected so that the notes flow together; in other words, the opposite of staccato.

Always play in legato style unless dots are shown to indicate staccato.

TIP

Legato does not come naturally to most piano players, so you'll want to practice this piece over and over. When you play a piece that's marked "legato," both you and your audience should feel the connection of one note to the other, as if each note is dripping over onto the next.

Playing Staccato and Legato

Practice both staccato and legato in the piece called "Hot Staccato." Play slowly at first, and then speed up as your skills improve. Also use this exercise to practice looking ahead as you read music, so that you're ready for any changes the music may throw at you.

A second exercise is called "In the Choir." You will be looking at four-part harmony (discussed in Chapter 7) and getting used to looking at four different notes at one time.

Your third staccato and legato exercise is called "Singing in F." It contains alternating sections of legato and staccato.

CONTINUED ON NEXT PAGE

In the Choir

Singing in F

Piano

legato *staccato*

staccato *staccato*

Repeat Signs

In order to avoid having to write extra music, arrangers use *repeat signs*. Two small dots appear at the end of the section to be repeated, telling you to go back to the section you've just played and repeat it. The second ending enables you to go on and finish the piece.

First and Second Endings

After repeating the section, you will come to a *first ending* and a *second ending*. When you play through the piece the first time, you take the first ending where the small dots are located. After playing the section a second time, you play the second ending, and then proceed to the end of the piece.

D.C. Al Fine

D.C. stands for *da capo,* which means the head or top of the piece. If you see *D.C. al Fine* written at the end of a piece, it means that you go back to the beginning, play the piece again, and finish at the end of the measure that has *Fine* (pronounced fee-nay; which means "end") written over it. When you play the piece called "Playing from the Head," look for both the D.C. al Fine and Fine signs.

Playing from the Head

CONTINUED ON NEXT PAGE

D.S. Al Fine

D.S. stands for *dal segno*, which means "the sign." Composers and arrangers use *D.S. al Fine* (literally, "the sign to the end") to indicate that a section of music should be repeated, without them having to write out that section all over again. The Italian phrase is indicated at the end of the piece and tells you to go back to wherever the sign (a symbol that looks like a squiggly line with a dot on either side of it) is written. The sign can be put anywhere the composer or arranger wants it. When you see D.S. al Fine, go back to the symbol and play from there to the measure where the Fine is written.

Now play your piece called "Saving Time" and watch for the D.S. al Fine and Fine signs.

Coda

A *coda* (sometimes called a *tag*) is the ending section of the composition. This can be written in any number of ways, depending on the arranger's choice. A coda creates a strong finish to the piece.

As you play "A Piece of Coda," notice the D.C. al Coda and follow the directions. You'll play to the D.C. al Coda, and then go back to the beginning and play until the Coda sign appears (in measure 8). At that point, you jump to the coda in measure 13.

A Piece of Coda

You may want to review the terms in Chapter 4 before moving on to the exercises in this section.

Terms You Need to Know

ACCELERANDO

Accelerando means with increasing speed. When you see this term, gradually (not suddenly) increase the tempo of the music.

A TEMPO

A tempo (pronounced ah temp-oh) tells you to resume tempo after you have observed a ritardando marking.

CRESCENDO AND DECRESCENDO

See Chapter 4 for an explanation and examples of *crescendo,* meaning to grow louder, and *decrescendo,* meaning to grow softer. "Let Me Call You Sweetheart," on p. 170, is a good example of playing crescendo and decrescendo.

RITARDANDO

Ritardando, labeled *rit.,* means to slow down for a particular section or until the end of the piece.

TACET

The word *tacet* indicates an area in the music where you do not play. In arrangements where other instruments are playing, there may be a need for a particular instrument to tacet (rest). This often happens in multi-movement or multi-sectioned works, where the tacet may apply for a whole section. When you see notes to play, the tacet is over. Try the piece called "Play This Tacet" for examples of tacets.

Play This Tacet

CONTINUED ON NEXT PAGE

Let Me Call You Sweetheart

Triplets

A *triplet* is a group of three notes of equal value that is played in the time value of *one* note that equals the same count. Slowly say the word tri-pul-et, and you will hear the correct sound of the rhythm. Some of the music from the 1950s and '60s used triplets in their style.

Triplets are indicated on the music with a number "3" over three barred notes, as shown in "Play Your Triplets," an exercise in triplets. In the first measure, the triplets are on beats 1 and 2 of the 4-beat measure.

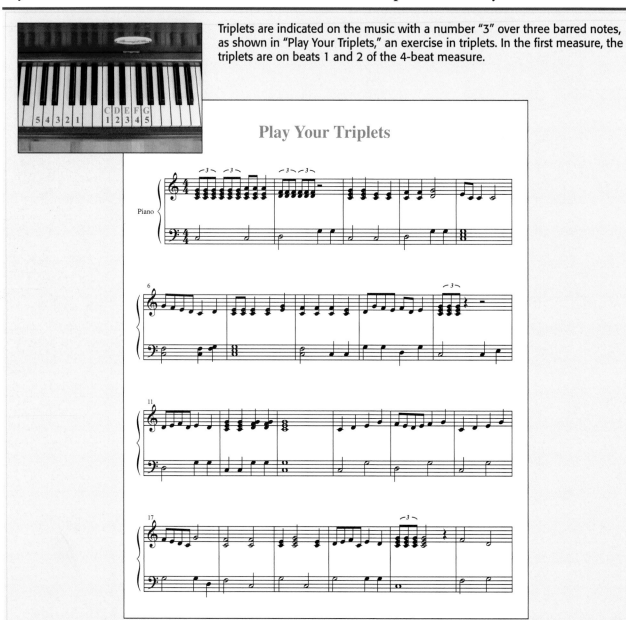

Play Your Triplets

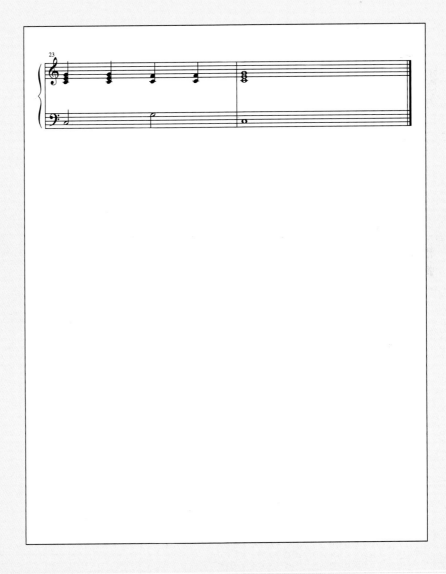

Additional Exercises

The exercises in this section help you practice what you've learned thus far.

"French Dance" is relatively easy to read and play, but it will be great practice if you're able to bring it up to a moderate tempo. Be sure to play the left-hand warm-up piece first.

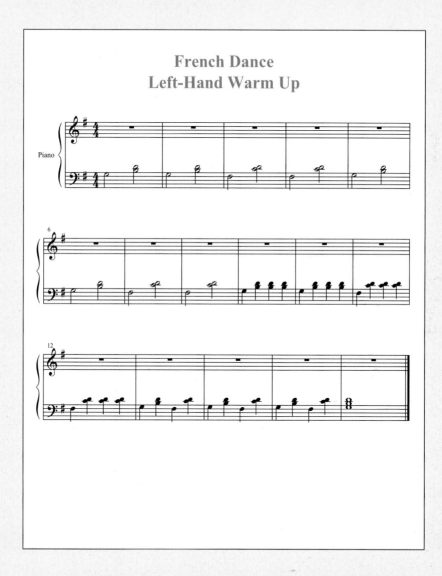

French Dance
Left-Hand Warm Up

CONTINUED ON NEXT PAGE

*Left hand
placement*

*Right hand
placement*

French Dance

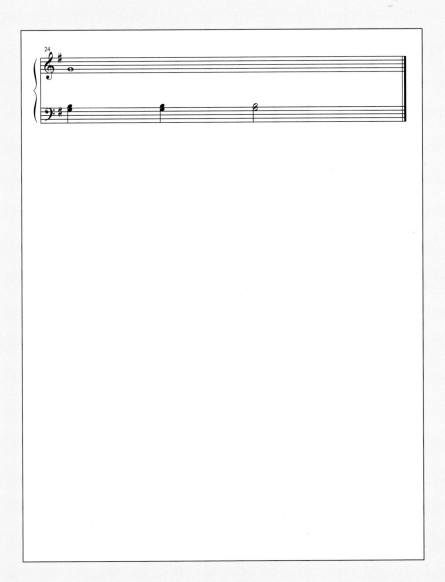

CONTINUED ON NEXT PAGE

In "The Evening Song," the term *lento* means slowly (see Chapter 4). Because this is a song about the quiet time of evening, playing this slowly is very appropriate. Practice with your hands apart first, and then proceed to putting them together when you're ready.

The Evening Song

chapter 9

Advanced Chords

As you discover in Chapter 6, triads are the basic building blocks for chords. But when you can play advanced chords, you can embellish the sounds and get much more out of your piano playing.

In this chapter, you learn about major and minor keys and their relationship to each other. You'll find out how to memorize key signatures so that, when you first look at a piece of music, you know exactly which keys are flatted or sharped.

Then you'll move on to all sorts of advanced chords, focusing on those that are most commonly used in jazz and popular music.

When you're playing with one or more other musicians and playing *by ear* (that is, without written music), all of you need to be able to communicate in which key you're going to play each piece of music. By saying "Let's play in the key of F," everyone in the group then knows to flat all Bs. In this section, you discover the name for each key and correlate that name to which notes are sharped or flatted in the key signature.

Major Scales, Minor Scales, and the Circle of Fifths

MAJOR SCALES

A major scale is an eight-note scale, the notes of which are separated by whole steps, except for the intervals between the third and fourth notes and the seventh and eighth notes (whole step, whole step, half step, whole step, whole step, whole step, half step). The most common major scale is C Major, which is C, D, E, F, G, A, B, C. This is the only major scale that contains no sharps or flats.

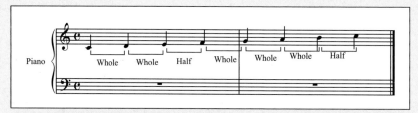

MINOR SCALES

The minor scale has the following pattern: whole step, half step, whole step, whole step, half step, whole step, whole step. The most common minor scale is A minor, which is A, B, C, D, E, F, G, A. This is the only minor scale with no sharps or flats.

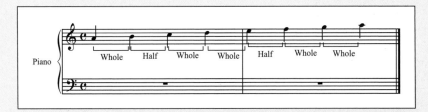

TIP

Keep in mind that minor scales also follow a pattern of whole and half steps, but it's not the same as the pattern used for major scales. A minor scale is a third (three half steps) below the corresponding major scale, for example C Major and A minor.

CONTINUED ON NEXT PAGE

THE CIRCLE OF FIFTHS: SHARPS

The Circle of Fifths (see figure at right) covers a five-note system for remembering the major keys with sharps in the key signature:

① Start in the key of C (which can also be called A minor), which has no sharps or flats.

② Go up seven half steps (that is, the interval of a fifth; hence the name, Circle of Fifths) from C on the keyboard, and you'll be on the G key. The key of G Major has one sharp (F♯) and no flats.

③ Starting on the G key, go up seven half steps on the keyboard, and you'll be on the D key. The key of D Major has two sharps (F♯ and C♯).

④ Starting on the D key, go up seven half steps on the keyboard, and you get to the A key. The key of A Major has three sharps (F♯, C♯, and G♯).

⑤ Starting on the A key, go up seven half steps on the keyboard, and you get to the E key. The key of E Major has four sharps (F♯, C♯, G♯, and D♯).

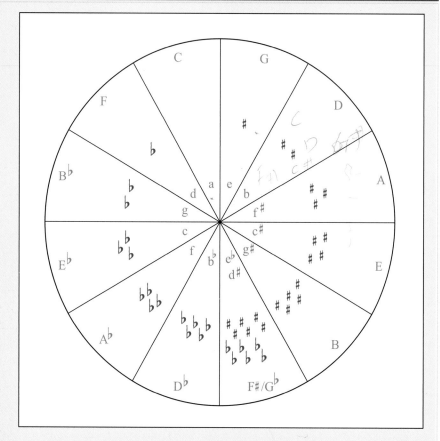

⑥ Starting on the E key, go up seven half steps on the keyboard, and you get to the B key. The key of B Major has five sharps (F♯, C♯, G♯, D♯, and A♯).

⑦ Starting on the B key, go up seven half steps on the keyboard, and you get to the F♯ key. The key of F♯ Major has six sharps (F♯, C♯, G♯, D♯, A♯, and E♯). The key of F♯ Major is also the key of G♭ Major, which has six flats (B♭, E♭, A♭, D♭, G♭, and C♭). Note that those sharps and flats are the same notes, just with different names. This concept is known as *enharmonics* and is discussed in more detail in Chapter 3.

So, as you can see from the sequence above, you add a new sharp key with each major and minor key as you go up a fifth (seven half steps):

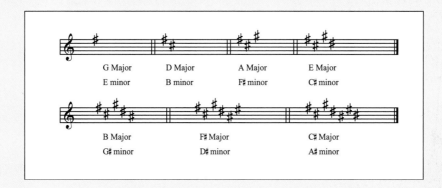

- From C Major, G Major adds F♯. The key signature of one sharp also works for the key of E minor.
- From G Major, D Major adds C♯. The key signature of two sharps also works for the key of B minor.
- From D Major, A Major adds G♯. The key signature of three sharps also works for the key of F♯ minor.
- From A Major, E Major adds D♯. The key signature of four sharps also works for the key of C♯ minor.
- From E Major, B Major adds A♯. The key signature of five sharps also works for the key of G♯ minor.
- From B Major, F♯ Major adds E♯. The key signature of six sharps also works for the key of D♯ minor.

THE CIRCLE OF FIFTHS: FLATS

There is also a system for remembering the major keys with flats in the key signature. You continue clockwise around the Circle of Fifths:

1 As you just learned, F♯ is the enharmonic of G♭. Starting on the G♭ key, go up seven half steps (that is, again, the interval of a fifth), and you get to the D♭ key. The key of D♭ Major has five flats (B♭, E♭, A♭, D♭, and G♭) and no sharps.

2 Starting on the D♭ key, go up seven half steps, and you get to the A♭ key. The key of A♭ Major has four flats (B♭, E♭, A♭, and D♭) and no sharps.

3 Starting on the A♭ key, go up seven half steps, and you get to the E♭ key. The key of E♭ Major has three flats (B♭, E♭, and A♭) and no sharps.

CONTINUED ON NEXT PAGE

4 Starting on the E♭ key, go up seven half steps, and you get to the B♭ key. The key of B♭ Major has two flats (B♭ and E♭) and no sharps.

5 Starting on the B♭ key, go up seven half steps, and you get to the F key. The key of F Major has one flat (B♭) and no sharps. So, you remove a flat key with each major key as you go up seven half steps:

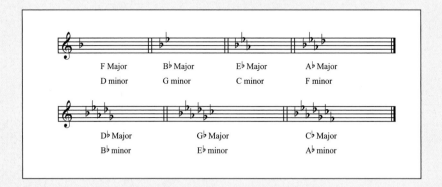

- G♭ Major (which is also F♯ Major with six sharps) has B♭, E♭, A♭, D♭, G♭, and C♭. The key signature of six flats also works for the key of E♭ minor (or D♯ minor with six sharps).

- From G♭ Major, D♭ Major removes C♭. The key signature of five flats also works for the key of B♭ minor.

- From D♭ Major, A♭ Major removes G♭. The key signature of four flats also works for the key of F minor.

- From A♭ Major, E♭ Major removes D♭. The key signature of three flats also works for the key of C minor.

- From E♭ Major, B♭ Major removes A♭. The key signature of two flats also works for the key of G minor.

- From B♭ Major, F Major removes E♭. The key signature of one flat also works for the key of D minor.

Now you get a chance to play some songs in minor keys. Start with "Frère Jacques," which is in F minor. Then play Beethoven's "Moonlight Sonata," which is in C minor. Finally, practice on Bach's "Fugue," which is in G minor.

Frère Jacques

CONTINUED ON NEXT PAGE

Moonlight Sonata

Beethoven

CONTINUED ON NEXT PAGE

Fugue

Bach

Major-Minor Triads: Building Thirds

A *triad* is the three notes together that form a chord: the root, the third, and the fifth. Using the C Major chord as an example, the *root* is the lowest note of the chord (C); the *third* is two whole steps above the root (E); and the *fifth* is a half step and a whole step above the third (G). (See Chapter 3 for more on half steps/whole steps and Chapter 6 for more information on chord basics.)

A *major third* can also be thought of as four half steps above the root (as in C to E, for example: C to C♯ is one half step, C♯ to D is the second half step, D to D♯ is the third half step, and D♯ to E is the fourth half step). A *minor third* is made up of three half steps (as in E to G, for example: E to F is the first half step, F to F♯ is the second half step, and F♯ to G is the third half step). Practice the major-minor drill to reinforce what you're learning about the major and minor thirds.

TIP

In order to play more difficult chords (such as those coming up in the remainder of this chapter), you need to know the structure of thirds. Both the sixth and the seventh grow from the basic triad (root-third-fifth) and add either another whole step or another third, respectively.

The example below shows you five groups of major-moving-to-minor triads: C Major to C minor, D Major to D minor, F Major to F minor, G Major to G minor, and A MZajor to A minor. Play each chord slowly, focusing on a measure at a time, and practice this drill over and over to reinforce these five major-minor chord groups. Also, keep in mind that although you're practicing with your right hand in this drill, most often, you'll be playing chords (accompaniment) with your left hand, and playing the melody with your right hand.

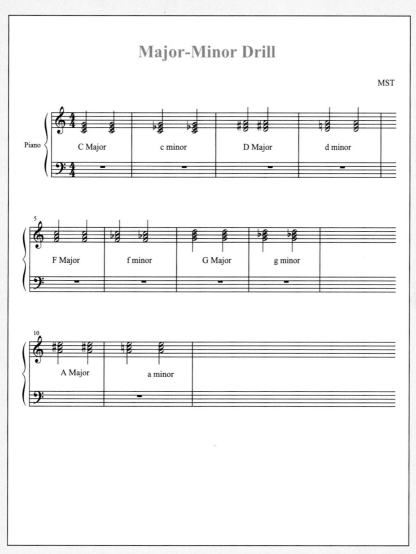

Major-Minor Drill

CONTINUED ON NEXT PAGE

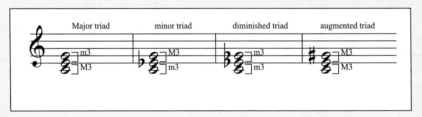

So, a triad is made up of a series of thirds. The *major triad* is made up of a major third plus a minor third, while a *minor triad* is made up of a minor third plus a major third. Here are some examples:

Major and Minor Triads	
Name of Triad	**Components**
C Major triad	Major third (C to E) + minor third (E to G)
C minor triad	Minor third (C to E♭) + major third (E♭ to G)
D Major triad	Major third (D to F♯) + minor third (F♯ to A♯)
D minor triad	Minor third (D to F) + major third (F to A)
F Major triad	Major third (F to A) + minor third (A to C)
F minor triad	Minor third (F to A♭) + major third (A♭ to C)
G Major triad	Major third (G to B) + minor third (B to D)
G minor triad	Minor third (G to B♭) + major third (B♭ to D)
A Major triad	Major third (A to C♯) + minor third (C♯ to E)
A minor triad	Minor third (A to C) + major third (C to E)

Also note two more definitions that you may hear. An *augmented triad* is a major third plus a major third. A *diminished triad* is a minor third plus a minor third.

The *suspended fourth chord* (also called the *sus4 chord*) gets its name because it takes the third of a chord and *suspends* it by raising it a half step to a fourth (hence the name of this type of chord), before *resolving* the chord back to its usual form. So, a Csus4 consists of C, F (instead of E), and G. The fourth (F) then moves back down to the third, which is E, thus resolving the chord back to the major triad (C, E, G).

Suspended Fourth Chords

Flat-Five Chord

In a *flat-five chord*, you *lower* the fifth one half step. So, for example, the major C triad is C, E, G, and the C flat five (or C♭5) is C, E, G♭ (which is the enharmonic of F♯, as it appears on the keyboard). This kind of chord can sound rather spooky. It's used a lot in pop and jazz music.

Use the "Flat-Five Chords" song to practice playing flat-five chords.

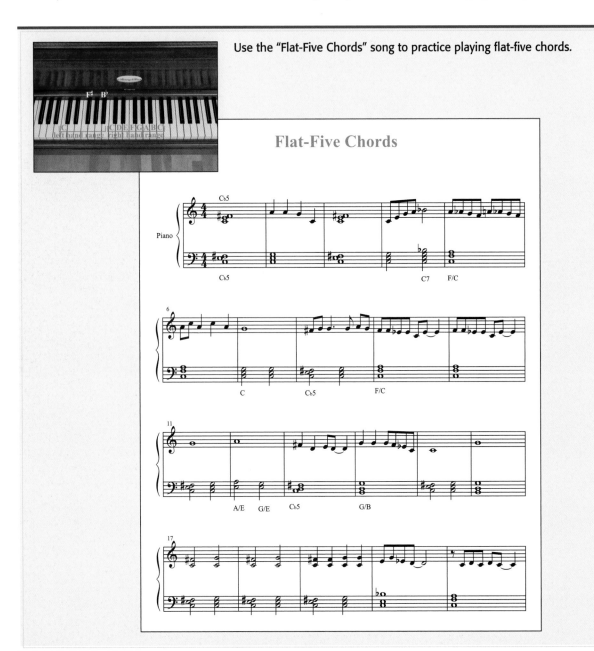

Flat-Five Chords

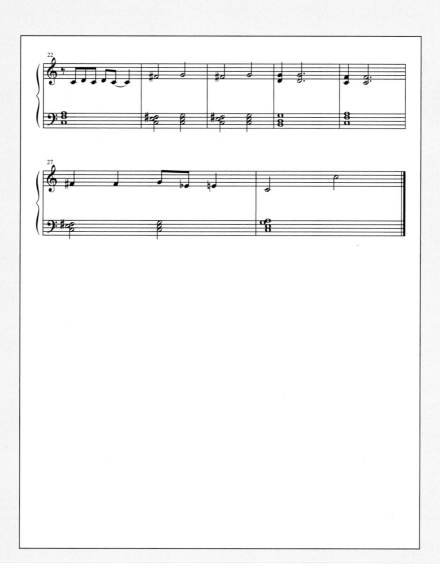

Sixth Chord

You construct a sixth chord by simply adding another note to a triad, one whole step above the fifth. For example, the C Major triad is C, E, G. The *C Major sixth chord* (also called CMaj6 or C6) is C, E, G, A.

You can have minor sixth chords, too. In this case, if you lower the E in the C Major sixth chord, you have the C minor sixth chord (also called Cmin6 or Cm6): C, E♭, G, A.

Play the piece called "Playing Sixth Chords" to practice the C Major sixth and C minor sixth chords.

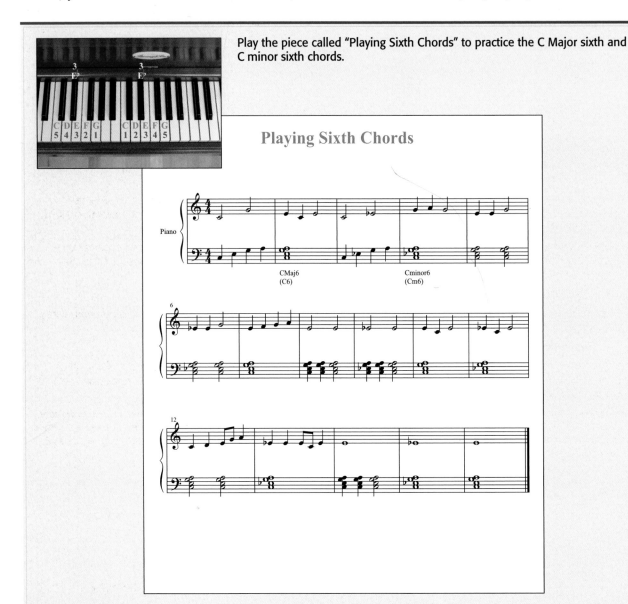

Playing Sixth Chords

The *seventh chord* adds a *seventh* to the triad of a root, a third, and a fifth. The seventh is another third above the fifth. The *C Major seventh chord*, for example, is C, E, G, B. That's a major third (C to E), plus a minor third (E to G), plus a major third (G to B).

Types of Seventh Chords

Let's start with the tonic chord and build seventh chords. A *tonic chord* is the prime or home chord. For example, the C Major chord is a tonic chord (C, E, G). It is the first chord of the C Major scale.

- The *dominant seventh chord* (also called V7) takes the tonic chord and lowers the root one whole step, raises the third one whole step, and keeps the fifth intact (for example, B, F, G). That's a major third, a minor third, and a minor third.

  Here's another way to think of it: The dominant seventh (V7) is a seventh chord built on the fifth note of the scale. In a C Major scale, that's G, B, D, F. It's called V7: V is the Roman numeral for five, because that's its scale position; 7 shows that it contains the interval of a seventh.

- The *minor seventh chord* is when the third and seventh are lowered a half step.

- The *diminished seventh* lowers the third a half step, and lowers the fifth and seventh one whole step each. That's a minor third, minor third, minor third.

- The *augmented seventh* raises the fifth a half step.

"Playing Seventh Chords" gives you a chance to practice these seventh chords. Don't worry about memorizing all of these definitions. Just practice the various types of seventh chords and become familiar with how they look on the music and sound when you play them.

Note: *There is another type of chord in "Playing Seventh Chords" that is not a seventh chord. The subdominant chord keeps the root of the tonic chord and raises the third and the fifth one half step and one whole step respectively (for example, C, F, A). Another way to think about it is that it is a second inversion chord built on the fourth (subdominant) note of the scale. In a C Major scale, that's F, A, C. For more on inversions, see Chapter 6.*

CONTINUED ON NEXT PAGE

The circles on the black keys show the accidentals in "Playing Seventh Chords."

A *chord dictionary* is just like a word dictionary but with chord explanations. These chords are written out on the staff for you to study and play them one at a time. This dictionary will serve as a reference sheet as you move into more and more expanded chords.

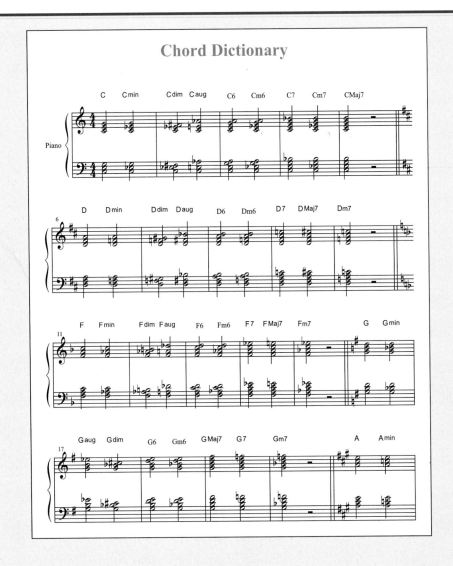

CONTINUED ON NEXT PAGE

Don't be nervous as you look at all the different chords. You will probably not be using most of them very much. The reason for having more chords than you are familiar with is because as you learn more piano you will most likely move into more and more expanded chords.

C Major

C minor

C diminished

C augmented

C6

Cm6

C7

CMaj7

Cm7

D Major

D minor

D diminished

D augmented

D6

Dm6

D7

DMaj7

Dm7

CONTINUED ON NEXT PAGE

F Major

F minor

F diminished

F augmented

F6

Fm6

F7

FMaj7

Fm7

G Major

G minor

G diminished

G augmented

G6

Gm6

G7

Gm7

GMaj7

CONTINUED ON NEXT PAGE

A Major

A minor

A diminished

A augmented

A6

Am6

A7

AMaj7

Am7

E Major

E minor

E diminished

E augmented

E6

Em6

E7

EMaj7

Em7

Playing Three Old Favorites

The three pieces in this section ("April Showers," "Alexander's Ragtime Band," and "God Bless America") help you practice everything you've learned in this chapter, including some rather challenging chords in the left hand. Take your time to learn each. Separate the chords into their individual notes, as necessary, until you can play all three or four notes together. When you've mastered the chords, practice the melodies with your right hand. Only after you're comfortable playing each hand separately will you want to put them together.

April Showers

A. Silvers
arr. MST

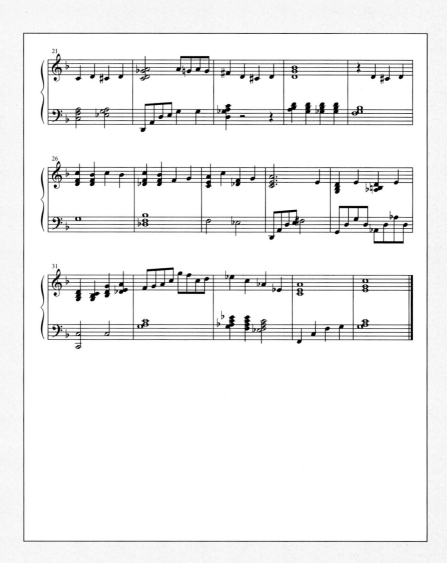

CONTINUED ON NEXT PAGE

Alexander's Ragtime Band

Irving Berlin
arr. MST

CONTINUED ON NEXT PAGE

God Bless America

Irving Berlin

chapter 10

Musical Styles

This chapter exposes you to many different types of music, giving you more choices of music to play as you progress in your piano education.

You find out about Scott Joplin and his influence on ragtime, and see ragtime's similarities to many different forms of jazz. You also get to play the blues, and you're exposed to a bit of boogie woogie to keep your family and friends dancing.

If you're into more modern styles of music, this chapter also gives you some country, rock 'n' roll, and new age pieces to play.

Finally, you find out how to improvise all of these styles to create a sound all your own. The chapter winds up by giving you an opportunity to write your own solo pieces.

Ragtime

Ragtime is a long-time favorite piano style that came from the New Orleans area. It's largely attributed to the pianist and composer Scott Joplin. Ragtime became popular in the early 1900s and was one of the forerunners of jazz.

Ragtime is dance-oriented and its rhythm is syncopated (see Chapter 4 for more on syncopation). In the practice piece called "My Ragtime Piece," you play the eighth notes evenly, as opposed to "swinging" the eighth notes, which is described in "The Blues" section later in this chapter. Also, observe the tied notes on the third beat, which provide the syncopation.

My Ragtime Piece

TIP

The origin of the word "ragtime" cannot be traced with any certainty. Some people, however, believe the word originated from the "ragged time" associated with the left hand of most ragtime pieces.

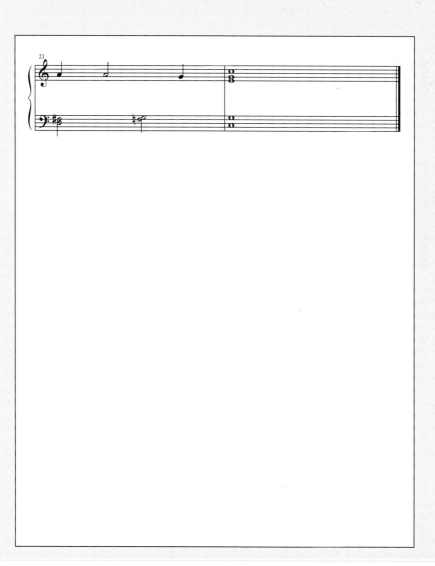

Jazz

Jazz, a favorite musical style of many Americans, can take many forms: New Orleans Dixieland, Free-form, Big Band, and so on. To play jazz, first you must learn some jazz elements that give it its distinctive flavor, such as the chromatic scale, jazz lines for the right hand, and the walking bass line.

Chromatic Scale

When starting out, it's best to follow given fingerings. The piece included here, "Playing a Chromatic Piece," features the chromatic scale. The *chromatic scale* is nothing but half steps, moving up and down. The chromatic scale is often used in jazz improvisations.

Playing a Chromatic Piece

Jazz Lines for Right Hand

Jazz Lines for Right Hand

CONTINUED ON NEXT PAGE

Jazz *(continued)*

Left-Hand Walking Bass

Most jazz bands have a rhythm section, which includes a drummer and a bass player. The bass enhances the piano with nice, deep notes, but sometimes it's not possible to have a bass. In such cases, the pianist plays his or her own bass lines and that's where the term *walking bass* comes in. A *left-hand walking bass* means that the left hand is playing the beats that would be supplied by the string bass in a jazz ensemble.

Play your left-hand walking bass notes, or *lines* as they are often called, in the piece called, "Walking Bass." The chords are written in the upper staff. See whether you can play the chord in each measure and hold it while your left hand plays the walking bass notes.

The Blues

The blues and jazz are closely linked, but the blues are usually slower and more somber, and the words, if any, speak about how we cope with various problems in our lives. The blues have a syncopated 4/4 rhythm, flatted thirds and sevenths, and a 12-bar structure (see the following section).

Play the practice piece called "Playing the Blues." In this piece (and with the blues in general), you want to swing your eighth notes. *Swinging* eighth notes means that you play a series of eighth notes as though they were a dotted eighth and a dotted sixteenth. This creates a ta-DAH sensation that's the hallmark of the blues.

Playing the Blues

Swinging Right-Hand Patterns: 12-Bar Blues

Twelve-bar blues is a style in which you use a combination of certain chords over 12 bars (measures) and repeat this as many times as you want.

The choice of right-hand melody patterns is based on the chords in the left hand. The 12-bar blues chordal structure is as follows:

First three measures: C chord
Fourth measure: C7 chord
Fifth and sixth measures: F chord
Seventh and eighth measures: C chord
Ninth and tenth measures: G chord
Eleventh and twelfth measures: C chord

See "Swinging Right-Hand Patterns" for an example—try your hand at it!

Swinging Right-Hand Patterns

CONTINUED ON NEXT PAGE

Now you're going to put left-hand chords together with right-hand solo 12-bar blues. Before beginning, practice the left-hand chords alone, moving back and forth between two chords to get the feel of the changes. Be sure to also swing the eighth notes.

12-Bar Blues

If you love to dance, boogie woogie style is perfect for you. It started in the late 1930s and continued into the 40s, when the big-band sound was becoming popular.

The form usually follows the 12-bar blues sequence, but it can vary, depending on how the composer arranged it.

In this style, you swing your eighth notes. You also move your left thumb up to the sixth note (meaning the interval of a sixth above the home key), rotating back and forth between these top notes. For example, in the piece "Boogie Woogie Piece," which is in the key of G, your left hand's fifth finger is on G, and your thumb is moving back and forth from D to E.

When you get to measures 13 through 18, you will play a new rhythm using a dotted quarter note followed by an eighth note and tied over to a half note. This is an example of syncopation. Practice tapping this section and following the counts, keeping in mind that a dotted quarter gets one and one-half counts, the eighth note gets the other half count, and the following half note gets two counts. (This adds up to the four counts in the measure.)

Here are some suggested finger placements through measure 9 of "Boogie Woogie Piece."

LH: measures 1 through 4

RH: measures 1 through 8

LH and RH: measures 5 and 6

LH and RH: measure 9

Boogie Woogie Piece

Country

Country music has an interesting history, because this music originally came from Ireland, Scotland, and Britain, and retains a little of Great Britain's folk style. Much of the country music scene is now focused on Nashville, Tennessee, but northern Georgia, East Tennessee, North Carolina, Virginia, and West Virginia (all combined, an area known as Appalachia), have produced a lot of country music, as well as bluegrass—a close cousin to country.

Playing this sound means using certain intervals that identify the country style. Using the interval of a third moving to a fourth is typical of the country sound. Also the interval of a fifth enters into the melody, giving a very distinct sound of harmony.

When singing, the technique of sliding your voice up and down is typical of a country song. Play your practice piece called "Play a Country Song in F."

Rock 'n' Roll

Rock 'n' roll is fun to listen to and dance to. It was popularized in the 1950s by Elvis Presley, and the Beatles didn't hurt the style, either!

Jerry Lee Lewis had a popular piano rock 'n' roll style, which included a gliss technique up and down the piano. A *gliss* (short for *glissando*) is when the pianist slides his fingers up and down the piano, touching all the white notes. To do this, you use four fingers, but not your thumb. Turn your hand over so that the front side of your fingers are facedown on the keys.

You hear the sound of syncopation in rock 'n' roll. Your practice piece, "Playing a Rock 'n' Roll Song," is in the key of G, so all Fs are sharped. Be sure to swing the eighth notes. Look closely at each dotted quarter note, followed by an eighth note and tied to a half note.

Playing a Rock 'n' Roll Song

New Age

One of the newest styles of music is new age, which gives listeners somewhat of a meditative feeling. It provides a mix of musical tones that are, at times, abstract from what you may be used to hearing. The mood of new age music is ethereal and light.

In new age music, the melody continues to repeat itself, and some of the sounds tend to overlap in tonality, unlike other music you've experienced in this book. Your new age piece, called "New Age Sounds," is in the key of F. Play it slowly with a legato (smooth and connected) technique. Observe the dynamics of mp, pp, and p (see Chapter 4).

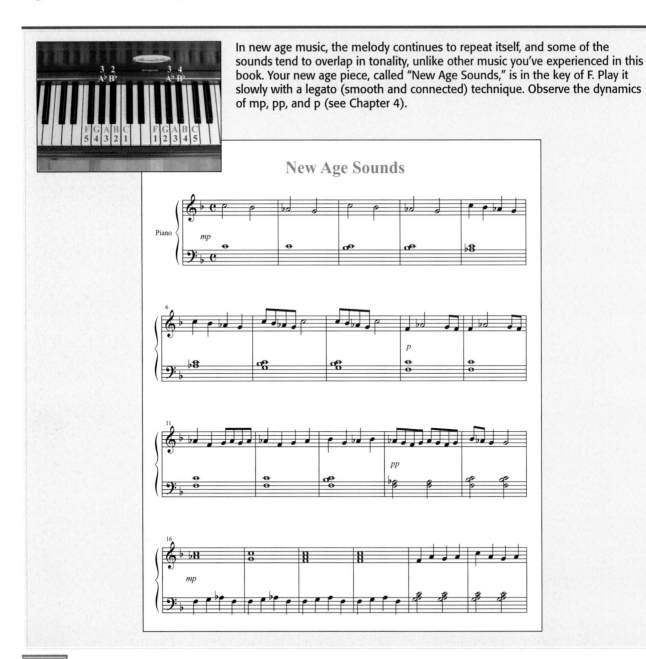

New Age Sounds

Improvising a Melody with Chords

When you create your own version of a song, without directly copying the original melody line of the song, you're *improvising*. To improvise, you take the content of the song—namely the combination of notes and chords that make up the tune—and you play around the original version of the song.

In your practice piece called, "Improvising a Melody," you see the original version for the first 12 measures, and then an improvised version. Look it over and notice how the first part of the song—the original melody—goes, and how the improvisational creation takes off on it. Then you have room to write your own improvisation. Or, if you want, write nothing there and make up a fresh improvisation every time you play this piece.

Improvising a Melody

Write your improvisation and use these chords

Making Up a Solo

Although this may seem daunting, it's time for you to write a song! You write and name the melody to go along with the chords given. It would be an extra bonus for you to add some dynamic markings such as *crescendo* and *decrescendo*; labels of shadings, such as *pp, mp, f,* and *mf*; *rit.*; *a tempo*; and so on.

A Solo in C

Start with simple notes until you're more and more aware of what works. Make sure your rhythm is correct (4/4 time) with the allowed count of notes per measure. Use a pencil because, as composers do, you will probably be editing along the way. The key and time signature will be given to you. This song should be written in the key of C.

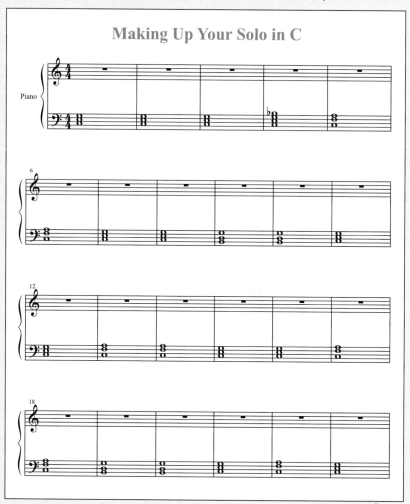

Making Up Your Solo in C

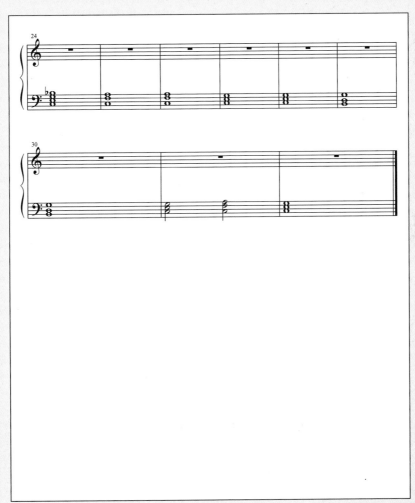

CONTINUED ON NEXT PAGE

Making Up a
Solo *(continued)*

A Solo in G

Here is another opportunity for you to write a song. This time, though, write it in the key of G and be sure to sharp any Fs that you put in your song. This piece is in the key of G and is a waltz in 3/4 time. (Be sure you remember there are only three beats allowed in each measure.) The notes in your song need to go with the notes in the chords.

Making Up Your Solo in G

CONTINUED ON NEXT PAGE

A Solo in F

Your last composition is in the key of F. All Bs are flatted, and the song is to be written in 4/4 time.

Now you are becoming a composer, right? You can go on to writing your own left-hand chords and right-hand melodies!

Making Up Your Solo in F

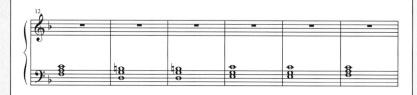

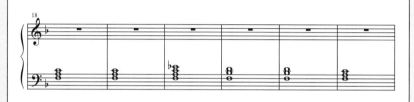

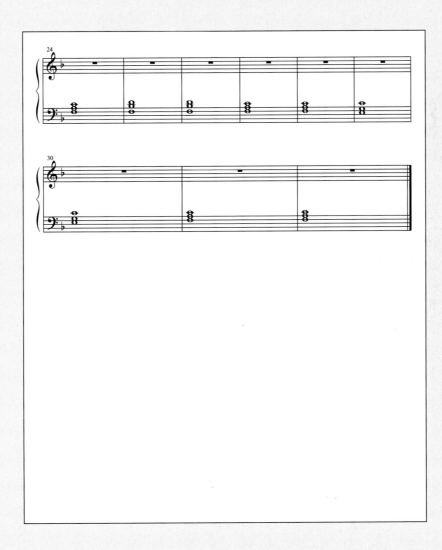

Appendix A

Additional Piano Pieces

Here are some more piano pieces for you to practice. These have been selected to help you master some of the techniques—such as staccato, four-part harmony, syncopation and walking bass—that you learned earlier in this book. You will also get a chance to work on some of the styles you learned, such as ragtime, blues, boogie-woogie, and country.

What a Day

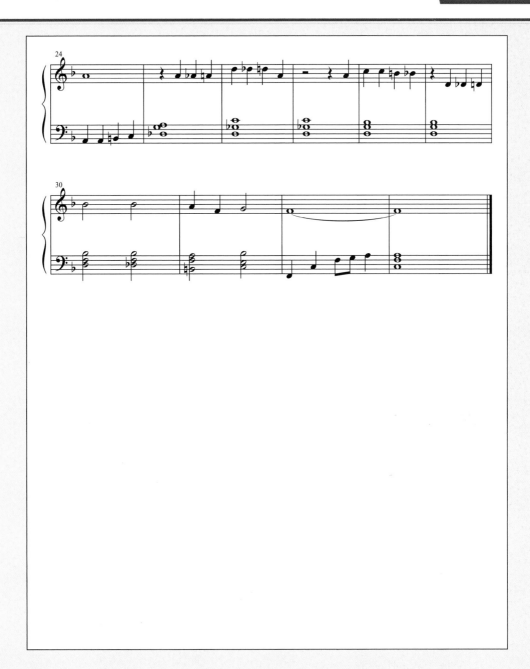

Spring in My Heart

America, Our Country

Let's Play a Latin Song

The Dogwood Rag

Jive It

Strutting with the Crowd

Piano

I Feel Blue

I Love the Boogie Beat

Why Can't I Find Love?

Für Elise Theme and Variations

Inspired by
Beethoven

Famous Composers, Pianists, and Compositions

Here are some biographical sketches of pianists you should know. You have already been introduced to some of them, but you should get to know them all. Most of these artists are/were composers as well, and recordings of their works are widely available at your local library or bookstore. We list here some famous piano compositions as well.

While we're on the subject, we encourage you to take advantage of any opportunity you have to listen to live concerts. It is a great way to gain appreciation for different styles of music, while supporting the arts. It's also a great way to relax!

Famous Pianists/ Composers

Johann Sebastian Bach (1685–1750) was one of the most famous Baroque Era composers. Although the pianoforte was a very young instrument during Bach's heyday, his compositions for the pianoforte's predecessors, the harpsichord and clavichord, have translated with ease to the piano. He wrote keyboard selections filled with counterpoint (notes and themes moving and developing in contrary motion); his *Well-Tempered Clavier* is a well known collection of such compositions. One of his most famous pieces is "Jesu Joy of Man's Desiring." Another well-known selection is "Prelude in C."

Burt Bacharach (born 1928), a jazz pianist born in Kansas City, Missouri, is best known as a songwriter and film composer, collaborating with lyricist Hal David on such popular songs of the 1960s as "Raindrops Keep Fallin' on My Head" (from the film *Butch Cassidy and the Sundance Kid*), "Walk on By," and "Do You Know the Way to San Jose?" In 1968, he and David produced the Broadway success *Promises, Promises;* other title songs for films include "What's New Pussycat?" and "Alfie."

"Count" Basie (1904–1984) was one of the most famous jazz pianists of the twentieth century. After playing with Bennie Moten's Kansas City Orchestra swing band, he formed his own Count Basie Orchestra, which was one of the premiere "big bands" of the late 1930s–1940s. Two songs for which he is best remembered are "1 O'Clock Jump" and "April in Paris."

Ludwig Van Beethoven (1770–1827) is one of the most famous composers of all time as well as an outstanding pianist. Many classical compositions came from his pen. His most famous piano selections are "Moonlight Sonata" and "Für Elise." He wrote nine symphonies, of which the third, fifth, and ninth are the most recognized. The well-known "Ode to Joy" is from *Beethoven's Ninth Symphony*.

Irving Berlin (1888–1989) was an immensely successful songwriter and composer of music for films (such as *Top Hat* and *Holiday Inn*) and musicals (*Annie Get Your Gun*), despite the fact he was mostly self taught. Some of his most famous songs include "Alexander's Ragtime Band, " "White Christmas," and "God Bless America," the latter popularized by singer Kate Smith.

Leonard Bernstein (1918–1990) was an American pianist, composer, and conductor. He wrote the Broadway shows *West Side Story, On the Town,* and *Candide,* as well as symphonies and his popular *Mass* of 1971. He was the conductor of the New York Philharmonic and an excellent piano soloist.

Victor Borge (1909–2000), an accomplished classically trained Danish, is best remembered for his comedy routines involving the piano. Of Jewish extraction, he came to the United States in 1940, becoming a U.S. citizen in 1948. His humorous 1-man shows on stage and television delighted audiences; he also performed seriously with U.S. orchestras and conducted performances of Mozart's opera *The Magic Flute* with the Cleveland Orchestra and the Royal Danish Theatre.

Johannes Brahms (1833–1897), famous nineteenth-century German pianist and composer, played piano in Hamburg taverns, while perfecting his compositional technique. He attracted the attention of Robert and Clara Schumann, who became his close friends and brought his music to the attention of the public. He composed four symphonies, a *German Requiem,* and much chamber music involving the piano, as well as many songs for piano and voice. One of his most loved songs is his Wiegenlied (lullaby), "Guten Abend, gut' Nacht."

Dave Brubeck (born 1920), a jazz pianist and composer, became very famous in the 1950s and 1960s with his recording of "Take Five." This was one of the first examples of playing jazz and improvising using five beats to a measure. His Dave Brubeck Quartet became famous for its innovative use of meter.

John Cage (1912–1992), twentieth-century composer and pianist, is remembered for his experimentalism. Such techniques as "prepared piano" (placing objects such as coins on a piano's strings so that its tone color is changed) and "indeterminacy" (composing in such a way that his pieces never sound the same way twice) earned him scholarly, if not popular acclaim.

Ray Charles (1930–2004), blind pianist and songwriter, was born in Georgia. He recorded the song "Georgia," and it became his most famous recording. He had a unique bluesy style of playing piano and was at home in the rhythm-and-blues genre; he also contributed to the country music genre.

Frédéric Chopin (1810–1849) was a child prodigy who composed almost exclusively for the piano in the Romantic style. Born in Poland, but living much of his short life in France, Chopin is known for his études, or short musical compositions that test a particular skill, along with ballades, waltzes, concertos, and other works; he also turned a Polish peasant dance into a serious artistic form with his Polonaises. His later years were spent in the company of novelist Aurore Dudevant, who wore men's clothing and wrote under the pen name George Sand.

Van Cliburn (born 1934) was the first American pianist to win the coveted First Prize at the international Tchaikovsky Competition in Moscow (1958). He performed with many U.S. orchestras and as a recitalist, specializing in the works of Tchaikovsky and Rachmaninoff. The Van Cliburn International Piano Competition, which is held every 4 years in Fort Worth, Texas, is his legacy.

Floyd Cramer (1933–1997) was a country pianist from the Tennessee hills whose famous recording is "Last Date." He created his own style of sliding from an interval of a fourth back to the interval of a third; this "slip-note" sound identified him with the public.

Claude Debussy (1862–1918) wrote many beautiful selections that evoke musically the same ideals that French Impressionist painters, such as Monet and Renoir, used in their paintings. Although his most famous piano composition was "Claire de Lune," he also wrote two books of piano preludes, and is perhaps best remembered for his orchestral tone poem, *Prelude to the Afternoon of a Faun.*

Eddy Duchin (1909–1951) was a pianist who led an elaborate orchestra and played for many society functions in New York. His famous song was "I'm Always Chasing Rainbows," which was taken from a classical composition. He died of leukemia at age 41.

"Duke Ellington" (1899–1974) was a great American bandleader and pianist of the Big Band Era. The Ellington Orchestra's members were renowned for their improvisatory skill and music-reading ability at a time when many jazz players could not read music. Many of the Duke's compositions are written in a cosmopolitan, smooth style. Two legendary pieces are "Mood Indigo" and "Sophisticated Lady."

Errol Garner (1921–1977) had an unusual style of playing that really set him apart. Both hands would not attack the notes at the same time, as is the usual case. Instead, his technique was to slightly delay the left hand when it played its entrance. His most famous recording, also written by him, is "Misty."

George Gershwin (1898–1937) wrote both popular music and concert music. *Rhapsody in Blue,* written in 1929, was one of his most famous compositions. He also composed the groundbreaking opera *Porgy and Bess* in 1935, along with several other Broadway musicals. This American composer's talent was endless.

Vladimir Horowitz (1903–1989) was one of the most famous pianists of the twentieth century. Born to a Ukrainian Jewish family, Horowitz came to the United States in 1928, where he played many sold-out concerts and made many recordings until the year before he died. He had an individual style and wrote his own transcriptions of famous piano and orchestral works by other composers. He was known for his manner of playing scales in octaves—faster than the eye could follow.

Billy Joel (born 1949) is a pianist and composer of pop music. A superstar from the 1970s to the 1990s, his famous songs include "Piano Man" and "Just the Way You Are."

Elton John (born 1947) is a British pop superstar who has composed and performed in all areas of show business. He is well known for his partnership with lyricist Bernie Taupin, which produced such piano-driven hits as "Your Song" and "Candle in the Wind." His most famous Broadway show is "The Lion King," based on the animated film. He is known for his flamboyant stage presence and lavish outfits.

Scott Joplin (1867–1917) was a wonderful American ragtime pianist and composer. His most famous compositions are "Maple Leaf Rag," which is credited with bringing ragtime style into the limelight, and "The Entertainer," which served as the theme song for the 1974 movie *The Sting,* starring Paul Newman and Robert Redford.

Liberace (1919–1987) was quite a showman with his heavily beaded capes and silver candelabra atop the piano. A classically trained pianist, he gained fame for his ornate style of piano playing through a 1950s television series and a popular stage show in Las Vegas. His most famous song was his rendition of "Till the End of Time," which was taken from a classical composition, Frederic Chopin's *Polonaise in A Flat.*

Franz Liszt (1811–1886) was a Hungarian piano virtuoso and a prolific composer, as wildly popular in his day as many rock stars and pop singers are today. He was the first musician to describe his concerts as *recitals*—a term which then caught on with other musicians, particularly pianists. He was called Abbé, having had minor orders conferred upon him by Pope Pius IX, but never became a priest or embraced celibacy (though he never married). He toured extensively in Europe and Russia, eventually settling in Weimar where he was an advocate of Richard Wagner's music. His daughter, Cosima, wife of conductor Hans von Bülow, eventually left her husband for Wagner and bore him two children. Liszt composed in every musical genre; and used the newly expanded keyboard of the nineteenth-century grand piano to great effect.

Thelonious Monk (1917–1982) was a jazz pianist and composer known for his improvisational style. He is the father of the bebop style and is known for his many collaborations with saxophonist John Coltrane. The album "Thelonious Monk Plays Duke Ellington," considered one of the classic jazz trio recordings, helped broaden his appeal with the popular audience.

Wolfgang Amadeus Mozart (1756–1791) was one of the most inventive composers and pianists in the world of classical music. Among his most famous works are *Rondo in C Major,* the opera *Don Giovanni,* and his last composition, *Requiem Mass in D Minor.*

Cole Porter (1891–1964) was a magnificent composer and pianist who wrote not only wonderful melodies but also all the lyrics to his songs. He was greatly involved in playing at New York society parties. His famous compositions, such as "Night and Day," "It's Delovely," and "Begin the Beguine," are from many Broadway shows.

Sergei Rachmaninoff (1873–1943), Russian piano virtuoso and composer, wrote primarily in the Russian Romantic tradition of Tchaikovsky (whom he met) at a time when many other composers had abandoned that style and were experimenting with other styles and techniques. Compositions such as his 4 concertos showcase the talent of the pianist, as do his various preludes and his *Variations on a Theme of Chopin.* He also wrote three symphonies and the famous orchestral work *Variations on a Theme of Paganini.*

Maurice Ravel (1875–1937) was a French composer and pianist. Although he considered it a trivial work, one of his most recognized compositions is *Bolero,* which was used in the movie *10,* starring Bo Derek and Dudley Moore. His virtuosic piano compositions include *Miroirs* and *Gaspard de la Nuit.*

Clara Wieck Schumann (1819–1896) was a nineteenth-century German pianist, teacher, and composer—all while raising a large family. She toured Europe before her marriage to Robert Schumann and again after his death, along with England and Russia. She was a member of the faculty of the Leipzig Conservatory and later the Hoch Conservatory in Frankfurt. Her character studies for piano are quite delightful; she also wrote a piano concerto and some piano chamber works.

Robert Schumann (1810–1856), a great German Romantic composer, strove to be a virtuoso pianist along the lines of Liszt, but damaged the fingers of his right hand by means of a mechanical device that was supposed to strengthen them. Turning to music criticism and composition, his music—which consists mostly of piano works, songs, and symphonies—is highly emotional and moody. He attempted suicide in 1854 by throwing himself into the Rhine River; he committed himself to a sanatorium and died there two years later.

George Shearing (born 1919) came to America from Britain in the 1940s with a unique sound that incorporated piano, guitar, vibes, drums, and bass. Everything was played in unison. His most famous song is "Lullaby of Birdland."

Art Tatum (1909–1956) was a gifted pianist who, unlike most jazz musicians, chose to improvise on chord progressions rather than melodies. He also liked to fill spaces in melodies with runs and other embellishments, making him difficult to accompany; most of his recordings feature Tatum alone.

Tchaikovsky, Piotr Ilyich (1840–1893) is known for his many orchestral works in the Russian Romantic vein, particularly his music for the ballets *Swan Lake, The Sleeping Beauty* and the perennial holiday favorite, *The Nutcracker.* His *Piano Concerto No. 1* was premiered in Boston and has become a staple of the piano repertoire. A tortured soul who tried to commit suicide on his wedding night by walking into a river, Tchaikovsky suffered from severe depression. It's hard to imagine that, however, when you listen to the beautiful melodies he composed.

Andrew Lloyd Webber (born 1948) is a fine pianist and a contemporary composer of music for Broadway productions. The most famous include *The Phantom of the Opera, Evita,* and *Cats.*

Chopsticks. This famous, easy two-hand children's piece dates back to the mid-nineteenth century. In 1877 it was published with the title "The Celebrated Chop Waltz" in England (no composer was credited), but it seems to have existed before then. It has been passed down through generations of pianists mostly by one young pianist teaching another. In France it is called "Cotelettes" ("cutlets"). Rimsky-Korsakov and Liszt contributed to a Russian collection based on the tune.

Clair de lune ("Moonlight"). Based on a poem by Paul Verlaine, "Clair de lune" is one of a set of four pieces for piano by French composer Claude Debussy. The set was called *Suite bergamasque*—named after an Italian dance.

Liebesträum. Liszt wrote three pieces by this name, which means "dream of love." Liebesträum No. 3 in A-flat Major for Piano, with its theme of earthly love, is a perennial favorite of audiences.

Malagueña. Written by Cuban composer Ernesto Lecuona in 1927. A malagueña is a dance in rapid triple meter from Málaga, Spain. It is similar to another Spanish dance, the fandango.

Minute Waltz. A piano solo written in 1846 by Frédéric Chopin. The actual time for a performance of this piece is closer to two minutes than one. It is said that Chopin was inspired to write this piece after watching a dog chase its tail; a nickname for this piece is the "Dog Waltz."

Moonlight Sonata. The popular title for Beethoven's piano sonata *Quasi una fantasia,* No. 2, op. 27 of 1801. In the key of C-sharp minor, the work opens with slow broken chords (arpeggios) that have reminded critics and audiences of moonlight on the water—hence the nickname.

Pathétique Sonata. This sonata, originally titled *Grande Sonate pathétique,* was composed by Beethoven in 1797–98. The adjective is not the "pathetic" of today; it was used at the time to describe what nineteenth-century listeners considered to be a heightened emotional contrast between the first movement's introduction and allegro. The Pathétique Sonata remains a favorite of audiences.

Rhapsody in Blue. A work for piano and orchestra, written in three weeks by a 25-year-old George Gershwin and orchestrated by Ferde Grofé. Its first performance was on February 12, 1924 by the 20-piece Paul Whiteman Orchestra with Gershwin at the piano. Because he hadn't had time to write out the piano part, Gershwin improvised some of the piano's part as he played. Thus, the piano solo at the first performance of *Rhapsody in Blue* likely differed from today's version.

Glossary

a tempo A phrase that tells you to resume tempo after you have observed a **ritardando** marking.

accelerando With increasing speed.

accidental A sharp or flat that isn't part of the key signature. When you see a sharp or flat symbol in front of a note, you must play that note sharp or flat for the entire measure, or until you see a natural sign in front of the same note later in the measure.

adagio Slowly.

allegro Lively; faster than **allegretto.**

allegretto At a quick pace.

andante A comfortable, walking tempo.

andantino A little faster than **andante.**

arpeggio The arpeggio, an Italian term for "in the style of a harp," is another name for a **broken chord.** Harp music is full of arpeggios.

augmented triad A major third plus a major third.

baby grand piano The smallest of the grand pianos.

bar lines Lines that separate one measure (bar) from another.

bass clef Also known as the F clef, this is the symbol on the bottom staff—the staff that presents the notes played by the left hand.

beat The count, a measurable unit of time in a measure. The time signature 4/4 has 4 beats to the measure.

bottom The far left side of the keyboard.

broken chord A chord in which the notes are separated. Another name for a broken chord is an **arpeggio.**

chord Three or more different notes played either simultaneously or in the arpeggiated "broken" style.

chord symbol A note name written above the treble clef on a lead sheet that tells you which notes to play in the left-hand chord.

circle of fifths A five-note system for remembering the major and minor keys with sharps or flats in the key signature.

coda A closing passage that ends some compositions.

common time 4/4 time, sometimes represented by a big C.

contrary motion A technique that involves moving your hands in opposite directions from each other, one hand going up the scale and the other going down.

crescendo To grow louder.

D.C. al Fine An instruction that tells you to go back to the beginning, play the piece again, and finish at the measure that has *Fine* written over it.

D.S. al Fine An instruction that tells you to repeat a section of music. When you encounter this phrase, you need to go back to the measure that has the D.S. symbol (a squiggly line with a dot on either side of it) over it and end with the measure indicated as the *Fine*.

da capo, or D.C. Literally means "from the head," meaning from the top (beginning) of a piece. See **D.C. al Fine.**

dal segno, or D.S. Italian for "from the sign." See **D.S. al Fine.**

damper pedal The right-most pedal that enables a pianist to sustain notes while playing. The damper pedal holds the dampers up, preventing them from dampening the strings.

dampers A mechanical device within the piano's body that lessens the vibration of the strings when you release pressure on a key.

decrescendo To grow softer.

diminished triad A minor third plus a minor third.

dotted half note A note that lasts three counts. It looks like a half note with a dot after it.

dynamics The loudness and softness of the music you're playing, as marked in the music.

eighth note A note that lasts one-half count.

enharmonics The flat equivalent of a sharped note (or vice versa); for instance, E flat is the same note as D sharp, and F sharp is the same as G flat.

fifth In a chord, the note that is a half step and a whole step above the third. It is also the fifth degree of a major or minor scale. In a C scale, the fifth degree is a G.

Fine Italian for "end" or close.

first ending The first ending appears near the end of a section of music to be repeated (indicated by a repeat sign). You play the first ending, go back to the beginning of the repeated section (indicated by an earlier repeat sign) and play through the section again. You won't play the first ending after you have repeated the section, but will instead skip to the **second ending.**

flat A symbol that tells you that a certain note is to be lowered by a half step. In most cases, this means that you will be playing the black key to the left of the respective note. A flat can appear in a key signature or as an accidental.

flat-five chord A chord in which the fifth is lowered by one half step.

forte Loud.

fortissimo Very loud.

glissando To slide your fingers up and down the piano, touching all the white keys.

grand piano Bigger than a baby grand but smaller than a concert grand, this is one of the horizontally strung pianos (as opposed to a vertical, "upright" piano).

grand (or great) staff In piano music, both written staves, the upper indicated by the treble clef (your right hand) and the lower indicated by the bass clef (your left hand) together.

half note A note that lasts two counts.

half step The distance from one key to the next, whether black or white. Most half steps are from a white key to a black key or vice versa.

hammers Covered with felt, the piano's hammers strike the strings, producing a sound when you press a key.

harmony A combination of tones that can either be soothing ("consonant") or jarring ("dissonant"). Harmony is a series of chords (considered vertically), while melody is series of notes (considered linearly).

high C The white key that is one octave (eight notes) up from middle C.

interval The distance between two notes.

inversion A technique in which you play the the root, the third, and the fifth of a chord, but put them in different positions, rather than that order.

key The physical white or black key on the piano keyboard; also the series of tones that comprise a major or minor scale, indicated at the beginning of the staff by the **key signature.**

key signature Sharps or flats that appear on certain lines or spaces at the beginning of the staff, just after the clef sign. These tell you what key the piece is written in.

largo Very slow.

lead sheet A piece of music that displays only the right-hand portion (that is, the melody), and letters above or below that indicate what chord the left hand should play (the harmony).

ledger line notes Notes that are written on their own extra little lines above or below the staff.

ledger lines The extra little lines above or below the staffs upon which notes that are too high or too low for the staffs are written.

left-hand walking bass When the left hand plays what a string bass would be playing: a group of varied jazz-like notes that produce the steady beat of this style.

legato A style of playing that is smooth and connected so that the notes flow together.

lento A much slower rate than largo, but faster than adagio.

lines Walking bass notes. Also, the lines on the staff, as opposed to the spaces.

loud pedal Another name for the **damper** pedal.

low C The white key that is one octave (eight notes) down from middle C.

major scale An eight-note scale, the notes of which are separated by whole steps, except for the intervals between the third and fourth notes and the seventh and eighth notes, which are half steps.

major third Four half steps (or two whole steps) above the root of a chord.

major triad A chord comprised of a major third plus a minor third.

manuscript paper The paper on which piano music is written.

measure A unit of **meter** represented by the notes and rests between two bar lines.

melody A linear arrangement of notes, as opposed to a vertical arrangement (chordal harmony). Many melodies are quite singable. It is usually the melody of a tune that you will remember, rather than its chord structure.

meter The arrangement of beats in a larger structure. In a meter of 4/4, every measure contains 4 counts in which the quarter note gets the beat ("is counted").

metronome A mechanical instrument that helps you keep a steady tempo.

mezzo forte Moderately loud.

mezzo piano Moderately soft.

middle C The white C key closest to the middle of the keyboard. In musical notation, it gets its own line between the two staffs.

minor scale A scale that has the following pattern: whole step, half step, whole step, whole step, half step, whole step, whole step.

minor third Three half steps (or a whole step and a half step) above the root.

minor triad A chord comprised of a minor third plus a major third.

moderato Moderate speed.

natural sign A sign that cancels out a sharp or flat.

note The symbol on the staff that stands for a particular key on the keyboard. Notes can be of various durations: whole note, half note, quarter note, etc.

octave An **interval** of an eighth. Middle C to high C, for instance, is an octave.

parallel motion A technique that involves moving both hands in the same direction, up or down.

pattern   Also called a "sequence," a pattern is a recognizable series of intervals that is repeated immediately after the original series, but higher or lower than the original series.

pedals   A lever at foot level below the keyboard, that enables the piano player to alter the vibration of the strings with his or her feet. There are three pedals on a piano the damper pedal, the soft pedal, and the sostenuto pedal.

phrase   A group of notes that expresses an idea.

pianissimo   Very soft.

piano   Soft.

pianoforte   Soft/loud. This is the "formal" name of today's piano.

pins   Little metal objects that are used to tune the strings.

pitch   The highness or lowness of a note, depending on the speed of sound wave vibrations.

play by ear   To play without written music.

playing position   How you situate yourself in front of a piano, before you begin playing. For good playing position, you want to sit facing the middle of the keyboard, with your feet flat on the floor within reach of the pedals, so that all the keys are within easy reach, You also want your knees under the keyboard, and your forearms parallel to the keyboard.

practice pedal   A pedal that many less expensive upright pianos have instead of a sostenuto pedal. The practice pedal muffles the sound produced by the piano, making it useful for apartment dwellers and others who don't want to disturb their neighbors.

presto   Very fast.

prestissimo   Even faster than presto.

quarter note   A note that lasts one count.

repeat sign   A sign that tells you to go back to the section you've just played and play it again.

rest   A symbol that tells you to observe silence. There is a rest equal to every note length: whole rests get as many counts as whole notes (four counts), half rests get as many as half notes (two counts), and so forth.

ritardando A word that tells you to slow down for a particular section or until the end of a piece.

root The lowest note of a chord.

second An interval that covers two white keys.

second ending After you have played a repeated section for the second time, you play the second ending, which allows you to go on toward the end of the piece.

sequence A sequence is another name for a **pattern** in music.

seventh chord A chord that adds a seventh to the triad of a root, a third, and a fifth. The seventh is another third above the fifth.

sforzando Suddenly loud or with a strong accent.

sharp A symbol that tells you that a certain note is to be raised by a half step. In most cases, this means that you will be playing the black key to the right of the respective note. Like its counterpart the flat, a sharp can appear in a key signature or as an accidental.

sight read To play something you haven't seen before.

signature There are two kinds of signatures, the key signature and the time signature. They appear at the beginning of piece and show you the key and meter to use until otherwise indicated.

sixth chord A chord in which another note is added to a triad, one whole step above the fifth.

soft pedal The left-most pedal that, on a grand piano, softens the sound of notes by shifting the keyboard slightly to the right to that the hammers hit one less string in the middle and high ranges. The soft pedal works differently on an upright piano but still softens the sound of the notes.

solid chord A chord in which all the tones of the chord are played simultaneously (as opposed to a **broken chord**).

sostenuto pedal The middle pedal that holds the dampers above a specific note or notes in order to sustain them. This pedal is used less often than the other two (see **damper pedal** and **soft pedal**).

sounding board An internal part of the piano that consists of the strings, pins, hammers, and dampers.

staccato Choppy and light. When you see a dot over or under a note, that note is to be played staccato; strike the key and then quickly lift your finger.

staff Each of the two sets of five lines and four spaces on which piano music is written. The lines and spaces represent notes on the piano. The upper set is for your right hand, and the lower staff is for your left hand.

step A unit of intervallic measurement up or down a scale. A half step up from C is C sharp. A whole step up from C is D.

strings On the piano, vibrating strings produce the tones. The thickest, longest strings produce the deepest and most resonant sounds, while the thinner, shorter strings produce higher, less resonant sounds.

suspended fourth chord Takes the third of a chord and suspends it by raising it one half step to a fourth before resolving the chord back to its usual form.

swinging eighth notes A pair of eighth notes played as though they were a dotted eighth and a sixteenth. Swinging eighth notes are a hallmark of the blues, among other styles.

syncopated pedaling Pushing a pedal after you've struck the keys.

syncopation The act of playing notes just before or just after a beat, or stressing a beat that normally isn't stressed. Syncopation is heard most often in ragtime, jazz, and Latin music.

tacet An area in the music where you do not play.

tag Another name for **coda.**

tempo The rate of the music's speed; how fast or slow to play.

tempo markings Words or metronome markings that indicate the rate of speed at which you should play a composition.

third An interval of three steps. A Major third is two whole steps above the root of a chord; a minor third is a whole step and a half step above the root.

tie A curved line that connects two notes of the same pitch. You don't play the second note; you just keep holding the first note for the number of beats indicated by the second note's time value.

time signature Two numbers, one on top of the other, that appear at the beginning of the staff just after the key signature. The top number tells you how many counts there are to a measure, and the bottom number tells you what kind of note gets one count. 4/4 is the most common time signature.

tonic chord The prime or home chord of a key.

top The far right side of the keyboard.

treble clef Also known as the G clef, this is the symbol on the top staff—the staff that presents the notes played by the right hand.

triad Three notes that together form a chord.

triplet A group of three notes of equal value that are played within the time value of one note.

una corda Italian for "one string"; another name for the soft pedal.

upbeat A note that appears before the first complete measure.

upright piano The vertically strung piano, as opposed to the grand (horizontally strung) piano.

value ratio The bottom number in a time signature. The most common value ratio is 4.

vivace Quickly; this term is equivalent to or a bit faster than allegro.

waltz time A meter that contains three beats to a measure, the meter that is used for the dance called the waltz.

whole note A note that lasts four counts.

whole step The distance between two keys (black or white), with one key (black or white) in between.

Index

Teach Yourself VISUALLY™ books...

Whether you want to knit, sew, or crochet...strum a guitar or play the piano...train a dog or create a scrapbook...make the most of Windows XP or touch up your Photoshop CS2 skills, Teach Yourself VISUALLY books get you into action instead of bogging you down in lengthy instructions. All Teach Yourself VISUALLY books are written by experts on the subject and feature:

- Hundreds of color photos or screenshots that demonstrate each step or skill

- Step-by-step instructions accompanying each photo
- FAQs that answer common questions and suggest solutions to common problems
- Information about each skill clearly presented on a two- or four-page spread so you can learn by seeing and doing
- A design that makes it easy to review a particular topic

Look for Teach Yourself VISUALLY books to help you learn a variety of skills—all with the proven visual learning approaches you enjoyed in this book.

0-7645-9641-1

Teach Yourself VISUALLY™ Crocheting

Picture yourself crocheting accessories, garments, and great home décor items. It's a relaxing hobby, and this is the relaxing way to learn! This Visual guide *shows* you the basics, beginning with the tools and materials needed and the basic stitches, then progresses through following patterns, creating motifs and fun shapes, and finishing details. A variety of patterns gets you started, and more advanced patterns get you hooked!

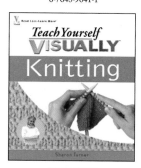

0-7645-9640-3

Teach Yourself VISUALLY™ Knitting

Get yourself some yarn and needles and get clicking! This Visual guide *shows* you the basics of knitting—photo by photo and stitch by stitch. You begin with the basic knit and purl patterns and advance to bobbles, knots, cables, openwork, and finishing techniques—knitting as you go. With fun, innovative patterns from top designer Sharon Turner, you'll be creating masterpieces in no time!

0-7645-9642-X

Teach Yourself VISUALLY™ Guitar

Pick up this book and a guitar and start strumming! *Teach Yourself VISUALLY Guitar* shows you the basics photo by photo and note by note. You begin with essential chords and techniques and progress through suspensions, bass runs, hammer-ons, and barre chords. As you learn to read chord charts, tablature, and lead sheets, you can play any number of songs, from rock to folk to country. The chord chart and scale appendices are ready references for use long after you master the basics.

designed for visual learners like you!

0-7645-7927-4

Teach Yourself VISUALLY™ Windows® XP, 2nd Edition

Clear step-by-step screenshots *show* you how to tackle more than 150 Windows XP tasks. Learn how to draw, fill, and edit shapes, set up and secure an Internet account, load images from a digital camera, copy tracks from music CDs, defragment your hard drive, and more.

0-7645-8840-0

Teach Yourself VISUALLY™ Photoshop® CS2

Clear step-by-step screenshots *show* you how to tackle more than 150 Photoshop CS2 tasks. Learn how to import images from digital cameras, repair damaged photos, browse and sort images in Bridge, change image size and resolution, paint and draw with color, create duotone images, apply layer and filter effects, and more.

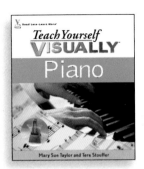